HINDU-CHRISTIAN MEETING POINT

OTHER BOOKS BY ABHISHIKTANANDA
published by I.S.P.C.K.

Prayer

In Spirit and Truth : an essay on prayer and life

Saccidananda : a Christian Approach to Advaitic Experience

The Secret of Arunachala: a Christian Hermit on Shiva's Holy Mountain

Guru and Disciple : an encounter with Sri Gnanananda, a contempory Spiritual Master

The Mountain of the Lord : Pilgrimage to Gangotri

The Further Shore

BOOKS ON ABHISHIKTANANDA

Swami Abhishiktananda : his life told through his letters (J. Stuart)

Swami Abhishiktananda : the Man and his Message (ed. Vandana)

Hindu-Christian Meeting Point

Within the Cave of the Heart

ABHISHIKTĀNANDA

ISPCK

This book was first published in French (*La rencontre de l'hindouisme et du christianisme*) by Editions du Seuil, Paris, in 1965.

The English translation by Sara Grant, r.s.c.j., was published in 1969 by the Institute of Indian Culture, Bombay, and the Christian Institute for the Study of Religion and Society, Bangalore.

The present edition, revised according to a copy prepared by the author, is published by I.S.P.C.K., Post Box 1585, Kashmere Gate, Delhi 110006. The permission to undertake this revised edition has been granted by the previous publishers, and is hereby gratefully acknowledged.

Ist English edition 1969
Revised edition, 1976
Reprinted 1984
Reprinted 1997

© Editions du Seuil, 1966

CONTENTS

Chapter		Page
	Translator's Foreword	vii
	Introduction	xi
1	A Catholic Ecumenism	1
2	From the Kavery to the Himalayas	8
3	Return to the Sources	26
4	The Gentiles in the Bible	34
5	The Intuitions of the Rishis	46
6	The Johannine Upanishads	77
7	Some problems discussed	94
8	In the presence of the Mystery	112
	Appendix	124
	Index	125

TRANSLATOR'S FOREWORD (1976)

ALTHOUGH the dialogues which gave rise to this book took place in 1963, and some even before that, its contents have not lost their relevance. It has therefore seemed worth while to issue a new edition, making use of the annotated copy left behind by the author in view of such an eventuality.

The Church in India has begun to realize with a keen sense of urgency the need to integrate the spiritual values of Hinduism into her own life. A number of books are now appearing on this subject, but nothing so far, it would seem, that can take the place of Abhishiktānandaji's book. Its special interest lies in that it takes us to the sources of both religions—the Upanishads and the Bible—and its aim is strictly practical: we go to the Upanishads to understand the Advaita and to the Bible to discover how the Advaitic experience can be related to the Christian revelation. In so doing we are led through certain passages of the New Testament, and especially of the Gospel of John, to what can, one feels, be described as an authentic Christian culmination of the Advaitic experience.

This Advaitic experience is first of all an experience of interiority. This cannot be sufficiently stressed today when a tidal wave of activism threatens to engulf the world. It draws man back continually to what is most inward in himself, to the 'cave of the heart' as the Upanishads call it, where God dwells, not as in a tabernacle, within and yet separated from man, but as the living Source of his being, of his very "I". At the height—or in the depth—of this experience, the soul of man is so overwhelmed by the glory of the Presence that his own finite self seems to vanish altogether in its splendour.

Christians are often afraid of this experience because it appears to threaten the radical distinction between God and the creature which is so strongly affirmed by the Bible and, we may add, man's instinctive craving for autonomy, yet we cannot ignore the witness of the rishis of India who have described it so persistently with the conviction of men who know of what they are speaking. It is moreover clear that if this experience has been more common in India than in other parts of the world, it is not confined to Indians but would rather seem to be something possible in principle for any man; though some may be more disposed to it than others by a keener 'metaphysical hunger'—the supreme *praeparatio evangelica* on the metaphysical level of the human spirit groping towards pure awareness of the mystery of God in which it is called to share by the twofold gift of nature and of grace. Since grace does not destroy but perfect nature, one would expect to find no contradiction here (which does not mean no Paschal mystery of death and resurrection), and in fact the Advaitic experience seems to open up new depths in man, so creating in him a profounder capacity for the gift of grace.

Only in the cave of the heart can true dialogue between Christianity and Hinduism take place; contact at any other level can never be more than superficial and fleeting. Too often in the past Christians have given the impression that they were not even aware of the existence of this space within the secret place of the heart (cp. Ch. Up., 8.1.1-6) where resides the supreme Bliss (cp.Taitt. Up., 2.9); and too often, perhaps, the impression was true. Now, however, the time has come for Christians and Hindus to recognize in each other the gift of the Spirit, and for that both must go silently down to the depths of their own being, to "the place where the glory dwelleth".

We are still awaiting a theological study of this theme — the author is the first to insist that this is not a scholarly treatise. Its role is to open up vistas, to awaken the Christians of India to the treasures of their double spiritual heritage, and so to contribute in some measure to the renewal of the Church in which the Spirit is so urgently demanding their collaboration. For he himself dwells in the the cave of the heart, and it is there that men must learn to listen to him and to each other.

It should perhaps be added that this message concerns, not only the Christians of India, but the whole People of God, indeed the whole human race, for in the economy of salvation the gifts of one are the gifts of all. It has already been noted that the Advaitic experience is not limited to those who are sons of India by birth. The special contribution that India is called upon to make to the Church may well be, as Abbé Monchanin loved to insist, this very awareness of the dimension of interiority which prepares the way for a deeper understanding of the role of the Holy Spirit in the life of the Church and of each Christian, and of the all-pervading, all-sustaining Mystery of God. The contemporary world, both eastern and western, in varied and sometimes disconcerting ways bears witness to man's ineradicable

Translator's Foreword

need for "That from which speech turns back, together with the mind being unable to reach it...." "He who knows the bliss of that Brahman," the Upanishad adds; "knows no fear. Every other creature lives by a small portion of that "Bliss" (cp. Taitt. Up., 2.9).

When some months before his death Swami Abhishiktānanda had experienced—so far, it would seem, as a man can experience it and live—that Reality of which both Upanishads and Gospel speak, he felt that what remained to him of life was given solely for the purpose of awakening others to awareness of the truth of their own Being. May this second edition of this book, which he himself had revised with typically painstaking care, be for many the occasion of just such an awakening.

Easter, 1976 SARA GRANT, r.s.c.j.

FOREWORD (1984)

Since 1976 there has been a steady growth of interest in the convergence of Hindu and Christian experience of the Mystery beyond all name, and theological studies are no longer lacking. It is enough to mention Raimundo Panikkar's *Myth, Faith and Hermeneutics* to indicate how far we have come from the first groping steps described in *Hindu-Christian Meeting Point*, Nevertheless it seemed worth bringing out this new edition if only to meet the continuing demand which seems to indicate that Swami Abhishiktānanda still has something to say here to the men and women of our time, more sophisticated perhaps than he in the things of the mind, but aware none the less that the final word is silence.

Easter, 1984 SARA GRANT, r.s.c.j

INTRODUCTION

DURING the days after Christmas 1963 a small group of Christians belonging to different denominations met at Nagpur to meditate together on the Upanishads. This was surely a sign that the Church had begun to discover the treasures which the Holy Spirit has laid up for her at the very heart of the great religions of the cosmic covenant.

The Church has always been aware that she is not restricted to the bounds which limit her in the eyes of men. Long ago the Fathers of the Church sensed her presence far beyond her visible borders, when they spoke of the 'Church of the Patriarchs', whose origins Gregory and Augustine traced back to Abraham, and even further, to the righteous man Abel. Throughout the ages and from one end of the earth to the other, men have been on pilgrimage towards the full and perfect revelation of her glory.

Isaiah in his day saw a vision of all the peoples of the world converging on the mountain of the Lord, bringing their treasures with them, to pay homage to the God of Israel. Yet neither the old Israel nor the new has any grounds for pride in being established on the holy mountain of the Lord—

> a mountain where God has chosen to live,
> where Yahweh is going to live for ever (Ps. 68:16)

If the nations are gathering about her it is not for her own sake. It is indeed her privilege to be a favourite daughter and beloved bride, but that should make her a more faithful handmaid of the Lord—just as Christ gave himself to be 'the servant of all'. The Church's role is to fulfil a ministry, *diakonia*. She was created solely to gather in the harvest of the Lord. If she were to glory in this, indulging in the triumphalism so vigorously condemned by the second Vatican Council, she would simply be usurping the place of her Master, and would fail completely in her mission.

The mission of service, to which she is called upon earth, consists in bringing together all men, all the sons of God—for all are sons in him who is the 'only begotten from the Father'—and to weave into a harmonious unity the hymn of praise which is God's due from his creation.

The great army of those who are 'called by God' is still on the march, converging from all sides on the place of 'assembly'* crossing the desert, advancing and retreating. and still experiencing the temptation to settle down in the oasis of Kadesh instead of pressing on to the goal. It is for the Church that has already arrived in the Promised Land and is assembled in Jerusalem, whose songs of praise even now resound in the Temple of the Lord, to summon home her children who are still wandering between the Red Sea and the Jordan. She must summon them, not as strangers or beggars to whom she would give alms, but as brothers, children born of the same Father, co-heirs with equal rights of inheritance. She must call them, saying like Pope John: "I am Joseph, your brother. All that the Lord has given me is yours. If he has brought me here before you, it was only for your sake." She does not covet their treasures for herself. All that she desires is that the whole heritage of the Father should at long last be gathered together, and that each of his children should be able to share joyfully in what is the common possesion of all.

The meeting of Christians at Nagpur at Christmas 1963 to read and ponder the Bible and the Upanishads within the fellowship of the Church, should be seen in the context of the Church's desire to enter into a genuinely religious dialogue with all men of faith.

No attempt has been made to give more than a brief outline of how the meeting came to be held, and a general sketch of the main lines followed by our discussions and reflections, as they developed out of our meditation on the Bible and the Upanishads during those days of grace—such indeed they were—days of grace and fraternal communion.

Each of the group would certainly have written this account in a different way. The results, while agreeing in essentials, would not have been identical in every point: for if every man lives by, with and for his brothers, nonetheless each one reacts in his own way, according to his temperament and his particular gifts. It is precisely in this that the glory of the Church'communion (*koinonia*) in love consists, being

---

* Such is the sense of the Hebrew word translated by the Greek *ekklesia*, Church. We may compare it to the *uttara sadhastha* of the Rig-Veda (1.154), first reached by Vishnu and destined to be the 'well-loved home' of all 'God-devoted men'.

Introduction

the visible reflection of the invisible life of the Trinity, which pours itself out in the variety and multiplicity of creation, and yet simultaneously flows back on itself, drawing all things to the bosom of the Father in the unity of the Spirit.

The responsibility for these reflections is therefore that of the author alone. He only hopes that he has not betrayed the general spirit of the meeting. He also hopes that any Hindus who may read these pages, will not be disconcerted by the theological position assumed by most of the discussions, which stressed the unique significance of Christ's incarnation; he trusts that instead they will look with sympathy on this sincere attempt at understanding the teachings of India's great seers. In any case, no one should expect to find here a merely comparative study or dispassionate evaluation, made from some 'outside' standpoint. Indeed, for faith no such 'outside' position is possible. A living faith is necessarily embodied in particular expressions of faith and any attempt to examine faith from what claims to be a merely philosophical point of view, inevitably implies a judgment of value. Faith can only be recognized by faith, in the same way that only a *jñāni* understands a *jñāni*. It is only in the depth of their own spiritual experience that Christians and Hindus alike are able to understand each other's sacred books, and thereby to outgrow the limitations inherent in every particular tradition.

As it stands, this report may prove helpful to fellow-Christians in discovering the treasures hidden in India's ancient Scriptures, and even more, in that *guhā*,* or secret place of the heart, in which they were first heard. For this *guhā*, from which the Upanishads welled up as from a spring of living water, is the inmost heart of every man; and it is to that inner centre that the Christian is invited to penetrate under the guidance of the Spirit, to discover in its fullness the mystery of the ātman, the Self, which was glimpsed there by the rishis.

There in fact is the place of the ultimate encounter; there man's spirit is henceforth one with the Spirit of God, the Spirit who proceeds from the Father and is communicated by the Son, the Spirit who is that essential non-duality, *advaita*, which held India's seers spellbound, and who at the same time is perfect communion, flowing from the Father's heart and shared with us by his incarnate Son. There the Spirit, drawing us into the mystery of his own indivisible unity, teaches us to say to God: "Abba, Father!"

---

* *guhā*—crypt, cave; in its mystical use, the depths of the 'heart' or 'soul'.

1
A CATHOLIC ECUMENISM

AT last, after centuries of narrow 'communalism', the hour of Ecumenism has struck in the Church, and for this we can never be sufficiently thankful to the Lord. Christians have become aware in Christ of the scandal of their lack of unity. They have begun to work together effectively with a view to making visible in the world ("that the world may believe"; John 17:21) that mystery of unity which Christ came to share with us here on earth.

However, an even more important stage in the growth of the Church's catholicity is now in process of development. This was clearly indicated by the Holy Father at Pentecost 1964, when he announced the creation of a new Roman Secretariat which was to be responsible for the relations of the Church with the 'world religions'. This too was an ecumenical event; for the disunity of those who have been baptized in the name of the one Lord and in the unity of a single Spirit is not the only obstacle to the perfect catholicity or universality of the Church. The term 'ecumenism' has in modern times acquired a limited and almost sectarian sense, though etymologically it should imply the extension of the Church to the whole of the inhabited universe (Greek, *oikoumené*). The Church is of her nature 'Catholic' (Greek, *katholon*, universal) both by her calling and her institution; but she will not actually be Catholic for all to see, until she has finally integrated into the mystery of her own life all nations, all cultures and all languages (Rev. 7:9). Only then will she be able to sing in the name of the whole world the 'new song' of God and of the Lamb. This was certainly how Pope Paul VI understood the world 'Catholic' in his magnificent homily on that day of Pentecost.

The creation of the Conciliar Commission for the unity of Christians was a sign that the Roman Catholic Church recognized the presence of Christ, of true faith in Christ, and of the Spirit's sanctifying action, among all those who are baptized. Indeed it is no longer possible for any Christian to doubt the sincerity before God of fellow-Christians belonging to other Churches, or to deny the fact that it is precisely through their membership of those Christian communities that individuals come to faith in Christ and develop their life in the Spirit. In view of all this, it is the duty of all Christians to enter into sincere and loyal dialogue and to seek together, in humility and charity, the way to recover their lost unity, in fulfilment of Christ's last prayer.

In the same way the creation in Rome of a Pontifical Commission for World Religions looks like an official acknowledgment that God and his Christ are present among the 'Gentiles' too. Thus at long last Christians can recognize that the longing for God present in other religions, at least in its normal manifestations, is to be attributed to the Holy Spirit (and not to Satan—this would be the greatest of sins according to the Lord; see Mark 3:28-30!).

This does not however mean that the preaching of the Gospel must come to an end. The Lord's commission still holds in all its binding force, and will continue to hold until he has "gathered into one all the children of God who are scattered abroad" (John 11:52).

Nevertheless, in this process of of 'affiliating' all those who are already 'sons of God' in hope, the Church of Vatican II, as it emerges from a long and difficult period of theological reflection, no longer assumes, as it used to do, that all those who have not yet heard the Good News are on the way to perdition, deprived of grace and of all true love of God. She no longer considers that the missionary's task is to build everything afresh, using (if he must) the ruin of what was there before, and adapting himself to the language and customs of his hearers (if indeed he condescends to do so at all) only because of the cultural immaturity of those whom he wishes to lead into the fold of the Church.

No doubt, when a man comes to Christ, everything in a real sense is made new ("Behold, I make all things new", Rev. 21:5; "for the former things have passed away", 21:4). There is a new *covenant* (Jer. 31:31, quoted in Heb, 8:8), a new *man* (Eph. 4:24), a new *heart* (Ezek. 36:26), a new *name* (Rev. 2:17), and likewise a new *people*, a people whom God has made his own (1 Pet. 2:9), who once were 'not my people', but are now the people of God (Hos. 2:23). Entry into the Lord's sheepfold is a new *birth* (John 3:3). To 'pass over' into Christ and his Church, like the passing of Jesus from this world to his Father (John 13:1) of which it is the sign and ultimate fulfilment, is always an act of dying and rising again (Luke 24:46).

And yet he who died is the very same as he who is now alive, renewed, risen. That which was 'natural' *(psychikon, animale)* now is and will for ever be 'spiritual' (*pneumatikon, spiritale,* 1 Cor. 15:44ff), having been renewed in him "who was and is and is to come" (Rev. 4:8)—"the Lord of that which was and of that which will be, he who is today and will be tomorrow also", as the Kaṭha Upanishad mysteriously proclaims (4.13), anticipating the Epistle to the Hebrews (13:8). It is indeed this 'resurrection' that gives meaning to all that leads up to death. Just as time comes to fulfilment only in the *eschaton** to which it tends, so all that comes to be—and therefore passes away—will find its true being through sharing in the mystery of Christ's death, resurrection and entry into glory; for he is the Alpha and Omega, the beginning and end of all things, and therefore their final and only explanation.

A truly Christian and Catholic view of the religious traditions of the world will regard them in the light of their eschatological fulfilment, their perfection within the very fullness of Christ (Eph. 1:23). The Church, enlightened by the gift of faith, sees all things in the eternal radiance of the Word, and perceives already in the groping and uncertain expression of man's deepest longings the full and perfect revelation of their ultimate realization. In the first pale glow of dawn she sees the full brilliance of noon. She knows that the whole universe down to its smallest detail, each individual human being born into the world, the greatest civilizations and religions of mankind, have all come to be in response to the Father's creative word; all are destined to share through his Son in the glory that was his even before creation; and all are kept in existence, ordered and given movement and life by the Spirit who, in eternally bringing back all to the Father in the Son, firmly and gently guides all things to their fulfilment in the mystery of the Pleroma of the incarnate Word.

The Church thus realizes that her mission is not to lead to Christ their Saviour isolated and poverty-stricken individuals, sunk in deepest error and sin. With reverent wonder she finds that in the hearts of those to whom the name of the Lord is still unknown his Spirit is already at work, bringing them to fulfilment and resurrection. She sees that this is not in spite of, but precisely through the instrumentality of, their various religious traditions, their rituals and Scriptures, and the spiritual

---

*eschaton—the End, the 'end of the world', and so the ultimate realities which are spoken of symbolically as revealed at the end of time, though they may already be dimly discerned by faith. Hence 'eschatological', referring to what has to do with these ultimate realities.

vigour and thirst for renununciation which these have transmitted from generation to generation. Those whom it is the Church's mission to gather into the Pleroma of Christ are not mere individuals, but men and women who have been placed by God in particular civilizations and religious cultures, each endowed by the Lord of history with unique treasures which are slowly being brought to maturity by his indwelling Spirit in view of the 'fullness of time'.

The time is therefore ripe for the Church—indeed, for all Churches together—to enter into official contact with these religions. This means that she will no longer rest content with the private contacts with followers of the cosmic religions established by some of her members on their own initiative. Rather she will try to engage in direct dialogue with their accredited representatives, in the case of institutional religions, or at least with those whose personal competence and spiritual worth are such as to make them acceptable to their co-religionists as authentic interpreters of their beliefs and aspirations. In such a dialogue the Church will certainly invite her interlocutors to cooperate with her efforts to stem the tide of materialism which is sweeping over the world; but it is even more important that the faithful followers of Christ and of the great world religions should try to understand each other in a profound spirit of humility, sincerity and charity. Each will be aware of the irresistible attraction of the unfathomable mystery of God in the depths of his own being, and will recognize that the religious beliefs and practices of his neighbour are the outward signs of an awareness of that Presence and of a desire to respond to it that is closely akin to his own.

In any case it is certain that when the Church seeks to enter upon such a dialogue, the most serious problems of mutual comprehension will be met in her relations with the great religions of the Far East. With Islam and Judaism she has at least the clearly defined common heritage of Abraham's faith in the living God and a common background of Semitic and Mediterranean culture. It was therefore to be expected that the desire for mutual contact should first have been expressed in relation to these religions traditions. We may recall the response to the visit of Pope Paul VI to Jerusalem, and the words which were then spoken on both sides, evoking the affinities underlying the obvious differences.

It must however be confessed that once the Christian has crossed the frontiers of Western culture he feels ill at ease, and finds himself poorly equipped to understand religious values which have developed

A Catholic Ecumenism

in mental and spiritual climates other than his own. The reason for this is the historical fact that Christianity is deeply rooted on the one hand in the Semitic civilizations that prepared the way for the Gospel, and on the other in the Greco-Roman world, whose cultural, philosophical and juridical treasures it inherited, and whose external structures and patterns of thought and experience it could hardly help adopting.

The Oriental world, however, whether Hindu, Buddhist or Taoist, seems to have reacted to that experience of the indwelling Mystery which lies at the root of all genuine religion quite differently from the cultural and religious world of the Mediterranean. The characteristic religions which developed in these very different cultural settings seem indeed to have sprung from quite different areas of the human psyche like rivers which take their rise from a single watershed, but flow down opposite sides of the mountain because of the differing rock-formations encountered in the neighbourhood of their common source.

In India men have not felt the need to objectify, to project outside themselves, the mystery sensed in the depths of their own being and at the very heart of the universe. If this is ever done, it is only accepted as a purely provisional stage, as a temporary aid for one who is still 'on the way', in the same way as one might use a raft to cross a river or a taper to light a lamp. In the last resort, the spiritual man in India will not allow himself to name this mystery, the absolute Reality, still less to define it, to distinguish himself from it or to think of himself as apart from it or 'face to face' with it. For him adoration can only be expressed in a wordless 'recollection' at the heart of Being, in the experience of *sat–cid–ānanda* (Being–consciousness–bliss).

This is probably the main reason for the Church's failure to awaken any real response in the Hindu soul. In spite of the impressive efforts now being made to rediscover and manifest her true 'image', even the most 'open' statements made by European theologians and the richest and most promising Conciliar texts have little chance of being listened to and understood in India, since almost inevitably they are formulated in terms of the situations in which the Church finds herself in the West. One has only to recall the extremely moving pleas of the Council Fathers from Western Asia and Africa, and then to reflect that India is even further from the western world than Constantinople or Dar-es-Salaam. India's characteristic experience of the divine mystery and the faith which is based on the experience of her sages and on the sacred treasure of her Scriptures have led her into quite different spheres of thought and into quite other regions of religion and spirituality.

When he meets this experience, which has been handed down through countless ages and is still living in the hearts of the holy men of India, the Christian can only adore in reverent silence the mystery of God and the unsearchable ways of his providence. As long as he is still conditioned by his Western upbringing, he may well be disconcerted by the outward expression of this experience at the level of 'religion'—prayer, formularies, rites etc. But, if the Spirit has already communicated to him some awareness of the innermost depths of his own soul and has made him sensitive to the unfathomable silence of God, when he first comes into contact with the true spiritual tradition of India, the words which he reads or hears will awaken a profound response within him, as though they had been born from the depths of his own spiritual experience. Then, still unable to understand, much less explain, what is happening, he will find himself exclaiming "This is the finger of God!"—the finger of God who is the Holy Spirit, as the Fathers perceived in their meditation on the Gospel (cp. Matt. 12:28, Luke 11:20).

If the Church is really to enter into dialogue with Hinduism, it is absolutely essential that Christians should prepare themselves adequately; otherwise they will remain for ever incapable of establishing any effective contact with genuine representatives of Hinduism. A superficial acquaintance with the religious folklore of India is not enough, nor is a scientific study of her rites and traditions, nor even a merely intellectual knowledge, however profound, of her Scriptures and the writings of her spiritual masters. The Christian who desires to enter into contact with the Scriptures and the mystical tradition of India needs above all else an inward disposition—what the schoolmen called a *habitus*—of recollection and contemplation. He needs the 'knowledge' of those ultimate depths of the self, the 'cave of the heart', where the Mystery revealed itself to the awareness of the rishis. It is only here, in the secret place of the 'welling up', of the 'source', as Ramaṇa Maharshi called it in his *Upadeśa Sāram*, that a true dialogue can begin. At any other level religious dialogue with India will necessarily remain superficial and unfruitful.

It may perhaps be objected that at this level of the human spirit there is no possiblity of dialogue, since by definition all words and mental images are excluded. However, it is only when contact has been established at this level that a true and spontaneous dialogue can begin at the level where concepts are formed and words exchanged, because then it will spring directly from the essential encounter. The same is true of the 'encounter' with the sacred texts handed down by rishis and other sages—it can only take place in the depths of the heart. And it will take place in spite of distances of space or time, for only the flesh creates frontiers; in the Spirit all can meet—at least all those who have entered into the Spirit. Similarly in the closely related sphere of visual art—for in India art, no less than the written word, is the bearer of the sacred—the face-to-face encounter with the Mahādeva of the cave temple of Elephanta pierces to the very depths of the soul and communicates the vision of the unknown sculptor with the impact of direct experience.

This preparation for the meeting of Christianity and India demands that, in his study of the Bible and of his own tradition, the Christian will dwell with particular attention upon, and make himself increasingly sensitive to, those texts which open up to him the mystery of intimate union with God. This means that he must also allow himself to be drawn with the beloved disciple into the 'deep heart' of the Lord, where the secret of the eternal life which is 'in the bosom of the Father' is revealed.

2
FROM THE KAUVERY TO THE HIMALAYAS

THE meeting held at Nagpur after Christmas 1963 is to be understood in the context of this new ecumenism and of the call to the Church to enter upon a true dialogue with the spiritual tradition of India. This is what brought together a group of Christians with the common object of reading and meditating upon the Bible and the Upanishads.

Shantivanam

The Nagpur meeting, however, was not the first of its kind. Similar gatherings had taken place in the two previous years, at Almora and Rajpur, and even earlier, soon after the death in 1957 of Father Monchanin, at Shantivanam, an ashram in Tamil Nadu on the bank of the river Kauvery. The first meetings attracted little attention and the number of participants was small—several Benedictine monks set apart by their vocation for a life of contemplation, a lay friend who was a frequent visitor at the ashram, and a priest who, in full agreement with the mind of the Church in our times, was following his own contemplative vocation 'in the world' as a professor of philosophy and comparative religion. Nevertheless these occasion seemed rich in promise for the future.

In these conversations we were always concerned primarily with the highest level of mystical experience. Christians, Hindus, Muslims and Buddhists all testify to the reality of a supreme experience of the divine mystery to which the greatest of them attain. This undeniable fact necessarily poses a number of problems for the Christian. In the first place, perhaps, there are problems of apologetics; for, especially in a country like India which has such a rich spiritual and mystical tradition, the Church cannot hope to win a hearing from truly religious men and women unless she too at last makes up her mind to put the stress on the deepest values of her message and of her faith-experience. The problems in the theological sphere are even more serious. Surely Christians have a grave obligation to try to understand the presence of the Spirit beyond the frontiers which they are only too ready to fix as limits to his action, and above all to discover the relation between the experience which the Hindu regards as ultimate and the experience of the Christian mystic. Must not the ultimate experience of God be an experience of the mystery of the eternal generation of the Son in the depths of the Godhead and of the inexpressible 'non-duality' of Father and Son in the Spirit? But apart from revelation, is it possible to attain to this fullness of experience?—for "no one knows the Son except the Father, and no one knows the Father except the Son and anyone to whom the Son chooses to reveal him" (Matt. 11:27). However, India's mystical writers speak of 'plenitude' and an ultimate fulfilment, and it is not easy to reject their testimony.

No solution can be found to these problems if we confine ourselves to the conceptualizations of Christian theology, useful and even necessary as these are in their proper place. It is from within that we must seek to comprehend this double experience, trying to realize simultaneously in the depths of our own being both that experience of the ultimate 'non-duality' which the Vedāntin regards as the final goal of human life and the experience of divine sonship in the unity of the Spirit which lies at the heart of our Christian faith. Only so will we be able to formulate an adequate theology of the presence of God at the very source of man's personal existence, and so become capable of fruitful dialogue with our Hindu brothers. Solutions cannot be imposed *a priori*. The instinct of our faith may indeed lead us to sense, at the very beginning of our effort to understand, that the experience of non-duality by its very nature tends towards the experience of the Father. But we are not thereby dispensed from pursuing our inquiries—not so much rational as intuitive—until the formulations of our conceptual thinking at last harmonize with the mystery which is revealed in our inmost being. Only then will we be able to show our Hindu brethren that the Christian experience does not fall short of that of the Vedānta, but that, without in any way threatening the essential values of the Hindu experience, it reveals within it even greater depths of the unfathomable mystery of God.

These meetings at Shantivanam took place in the peace and silence of a palm grove near the quietly flowing river. The day began according to Benedictine custom with sung Lauds and Mass. One year, on Christmas Day, the whole group joined in singing the entire night office and the three Masses at midnight, dawn and noon.

In 1960 Shantivanam welcomed new guests. A providential contact between the Catholic ashram in the south and the ashram of Jyotiniketan in the north made it possible to invite to Shantivanam for a week of study and prayer a group of non-Catholic fellow Christians, most of them ordained ministers of their Churches—Anglicans, Presbyterians, Congregationlists, members of the Church of South India, and an archimandrite of the Russian Church. They came from ashrams, parishes and seminaries. Some were a little apprehensive at the prospect of crossing the threshold of a Roman Catholic ashram, but within a very short time all were completely at home. Proof of this was quickly forthcoming when even those who had cautiously arrived in formal European garb promptly shed it in favour of the simple Tamilian *veshti* or the northern *dhoti* which they had packed just in case...

The hospitality offered at Shantivanam was in the Tamil ashramite tradition. The guests slept, sat and took their meals on the ground, and the food was strictly vegetarian, as is the custom in an ashram. Morning and evening all gathered in the *mandapam* or portico of the chapel for prayer. This consisted of readings from the Bible, each followed by a psalm sung responsively and a prayer either read or improvised by one of those present. The morning prayer was followed by a sung Mass in which the Catholics of the village took part. The Epistle and Gospel were read first in Tamil, then in English. In the evening, after the reading of the Gospel and the Magnificat, the offering of light (*āratī*) was made according to Indian tradition, during which the *Trisagion* and the hymn *Phos Hilaron* were sung as at the ceremony of the *Lucernarium* in the Oriental Christian tradition. It was also in the same mandapam, with the doors of the sanctuary closed, that we took our midday and evening meals in the manner of an Agape, and while the rice was being served we sang a Sanskrit hymn to Christ adapted from the Upanishads.

We met together for discussion twice a day, always beginning with ten or fifteen minutes of silent meditation. Then one of us spoke briefly on the theme for the day, and discussion followed. These themes were always centred on the essential point—contemplative prayer, the most urgent need of the Church in India. Each one contributed his own experience, and the light he had received from his habitual meditation on the Word of God. Thus we spoke of prayer in its different forms, of worship and the Eucharist. One day the Orthodox member of the group introduced us to the greatness of the 'Jesus Prayer'. In the middle of the week we decided to observe complete silence from

From the Kauvery to the Himalaya

Compline one evening until the following afternoon, and this was certainly not the least fruitful period in our time together.

Wider Horizons

In January 1961 Dr J.-A. Cuttat, who had recently arrived in India as the Swiss Ambassador, expressed his desire to bring together a group of priests and theologians interested in the problem of 'dialogue in depth' between India and the Church. The experience of the gatherings at Shantivanam and the resulting contacts made it possible for this wish to be realized, and arrangements were made to meet in Easter week of the same year. The idea was to enable these theologians to get to know each other, so that they could freely exchange experiences and ideas, stimulate each other in their explorations and escape from the isolation which so easily breeds discouragement.

We had no intention of trying to formulate resolutions or arrive at final conclusions. The territory in which we were workding was far too little known for that; moreover, premature attempts at definition destroy spontaneity and sometimes lead into perilous paths. We realized that for this kind of work a long period of growth was necessary, and our desires and hopes were correspondingly modest. Our chief aim was to discover the main lines along which the Holy Spirit seemed to be leading India towards the Church, and equally, the Church towards India. We wanted to do this for our own sakes first of all, with a view to deepening our own contemplative life, without which no communication is possible in the world of grace. Even more, we wanted to do it for the Church, and especially for those Christians who are less free to undertake these investigations for themselves, and who live in more immediate contact with popular superstition and the ever-growing materialism of our times. In spite of all this, or rather, through this, they also must be helped to recognize the providential designs of the Lord for India and the ways in which he is calling all Christians to cooperate in their realization.

It was decided from the outset to confine these meetings to Christians. There could as yet be no question of beginning a group dialogue with representatives of Hindu thought and spirituality. Each of us, it is true, had had considerable contact with Hindus, though at very different levels, according to the particular circumstances of his vocation, and it was precisely the sharing of these experiences that gave our meetings their unique value. Nevertheless we were acutely conscious of our need for a more thorough preparation before we could think of meeting Hindus as a group officially representing the Christian Churches.

Every one knows how difficult it is to achieve an *epoché** however provisional, of one's own convictions, especially one's religious convictions. Yet this is the essential precondition of any true dialogue. Without it, it is impossible to find out what the other man really thinks or to understand his ideas in terms, not of one's own mental framework, but of his convictions and the basic principles on which they are built.

On the other hand, if either of the participants retreats behind his defences, and either relapses into total silence or emerges only to give battle, the atmosphere becomes impossible for dialogue.

It was agreed that the hoped-for meetings between Hindus and Christians should be kept quite distinct from those of our own exclusively Christian group, and that in planning the eventual Hindu-Christian discussions great care should be taken to see that the participants on both sides should be equally matched in all respects.

We also agreed that the meetings should be confined to persons who were anxious to engage in real dialogue as opposed to paralled monologues, and who would therefore show genuine interest in and consideration for each other. Above all, they should be particularly concerned to remain on a truly spiritual level, without straying into either intellectualism or sentimentality.

Almora

The first meeting of the group took place at Almora in April 1961. The Methodist Bishop of Delhi kindly lent us his house, and some friends who lived nearby saw to the preparations, including the catering. It must however be admitted that, though the position of the house was magnificent, its distance from the town created more than one problem on the material level. The site was indeed unique, and we have never since found its equal. For our morning Eucharist we gathered in front of the house under an immense deodar tree, having as 'backdrop' for the altar the almost unbelievable chain of snow-clad Himalayan peaks, touched with the light of the rising sun.

---

*Epoche, that is 'placing within brackets', 'keeping in abeyance', not to be confused with the 'methodic doubt' of Descartes. Husserl defines it as "a certain suspension of judgement which is combined with a conviction of the truth which remain unshaken." The use of the term in our context owes much to the writings and speeches of Dr J.–A. Cuttat.

From the Kauvery to the Himalaya

The decision to hold this meeting at such short notice left little time for detailed planning, and moreover no one felt that he had the right to impose on others his own ideas about hours of work, rest or free time. The result was that the inspiration of the more eloquent among us knew no restraint. Work-sessions encroached upon meal-times, and the hour set for the afternoon discussion period found us still engaged in conversation at the lunch-table. As for the prolongation of the evening sessions, the less said the better!

However, these interminable conversations never wandered away from the fundamental points that we had met to discuss—dialogue 'from within' between Hinduism and Christianity, reflection on the mystery of interiority which is so characteristic of the Indian approach to the divine, and the problem posed to Christianity by the existence of an authentic mystical experience outside its own apparent frontiers. All those who were present have very happy recollections of that simple and spontaneous sharing of thought and experience which enabled us really to *meet* each other and to deepen our mutual understanding to the point of recognizing ourselves in each other.

Despite the almost uninterrupted conversation there was a prevailing atmosphere of prayer. We were conscious of being in the Presence. There were no newspapers, no importunate visitors. Everything was centred on the one essential, in complete freedom and mutual trust. Indeed, contemplation of the immense solitude of the Himalayas, our permanent horizon, could not fail to create in us a deepening sense of the ultimate Mystery. It was in these very mountains, according to Indian tradition, that the rishis lived—those holy men who were the first to hear and reveal to their brothers that almost imperceptible murmur which sounds in the depth of the heart, like the murmur of the streams which wind through the Himalayan gorges, scarcely noticed by travellers along the higher slopes, but swelling continually as one descends towards the torrent, until at last it drowns every other sound in its overwhelming thunder...

The high point of our meeting was the day on which each one was invited to tell the others in a spirit of simplicity and fraternal union in the Lord, what he himself as a Christian had learnt in India, how India had helped him personally to understand better the Mystery of Christ— in a word, to describe the impact on his spiritual life of his encounter with India. The idea was not to reflect in an academic way on what India could or should contribute to Christian spirituality, but to say what in actual fact she had give to us whose vocation it was to travel as pilgrims along her paths in the course of our ascent of the mountain of the Lord.

One of us said he had first come into contact with India through books and also through some European friends of an esoteric bent. Through reading, meditation and the practice of yogic concentration he had become aware of hitherto unknown areas of the psyche, in which he had discovered a dimension of interiority, not merely psychic, but religous and still more spiritual, whose existence the bourgeois Christianity in which he had been brought up had not even led him to suspect. The confrontation between this superficial Christianity and the deeply spiritual Hinduism into which he was now initiated inevitably caused him to lose all interest in the rites, customs and conceptual formulations of his traditional religion. It was only later on, when he was introduced to Orthodox spirituality and above all to the Jesus Prayer, that he discovered in Christianity also those profound values which India had revealed to him and which, but for her, he would never have known. As he liked to say, grace had come to him through India.

Another confessed that he too, in his contact with the Scriptures and sages of India, had felt a sanse of vertigo, of losing his balance on the edge of the great abyss. But one day, in the very depths of that abyss of non-duality revealed to him by the Upanishads and the experience of the sages, where the soul and God are 'not two', he heard as though coming from an even deeper abyss the voice of the Father, calling him to be, in the Son, himself both son and creature... This invitation had revealed to him a secret of interiority which seemed to go beyond even that of the rishis, a secret whose existence could not even be guessed at apart from the revelation of the Trinitarian mystery: the interiority of the Spirit, who is the 'non-duality' of the Father and Son. "The Vedantic night," he concluded, "is certainly a royal road by which to enter into the ultimate secret of the mystery of the Blessed Trinity."

Someone else said that he had found in the life of Hindu monks a witness to the Absolute and a detachment whose equal he had never before met, except in the greatest of the Fathers of Christian monasticism. It seemed to him that through them God was calling him first of all to a more complete and more essential self-stripping within his own monastic tradition, and then perhaps even to a kind of monasticism, freed from the institutional forms imposed on it in the

West, which would seek to recover the spirit of the Desert Fathers, and which would at last bring the traditional *sannyāsa* of India to its eschatological fulfilment in the Church.

Yet another had arrived in India with all the paraphernalia deemed necessary by the missionary society to which he belonged. Then he came in contact with India's poor and with some disciples of Mahatma Gandhi who were serving them in humility and poverty, leading a life whose authenticity gave him pause. In these servants of the poor of India he seemed to rediscover the Gospel, the good news, the call to service and to love proclaimed by Christ to the Galilean crowds, which these people were living with a rare sincerity. He understood that Christ was already here, not yet known by the name revealed by the angel, but surely in the reality inspired by the Spirit. He realized then that it is not for us, in the self-conceit induced by our privileges as Westerners and Christians of long standing, to claim that we are 'bringing Christ to India'—in our luggage, as it were! If we truly wish to lead the people of India to the Paschal illumination of baptism and to the acceptance of the Church's testimony, we must first of all, whatever the cost, learn to share completely in the life of the common people, and to live out on their level the gospel of the Beatitudes, according to the instructions given by Jesus himself, when he sent out the seventy 'missionaries' to announce his coming (Luke 10:1–7). This then was the inspiration which had finally led him to live in prayer and service, poverty and humility, among poor and illiterate peasants on the banks of the Ram-Ganga.

Another of the group was living among Bengali professors and university students. He too had experienced very intensely the mystery of the One-without-a-second. In our discussion he protested vigorously whenever anyone used any expression to describe the relation between God and the creature which seemed to him to endanger that fundamental intuition or to border on an impossible dualism. However, what he shared with us that morning was the impression made on him by the piety, or *bhakti*, of the people among whom he was living, and the reverence with which they venerated the *mūrti*, the 'forms' under which the divinity is represented and worshipped in their temples. He helped us to understand the truth that is hidden in the 'worship of idols', which in India at least does not merit the denunciation launched by Israel's prophets at the cults of Canaan and Babylon. He explained to us the religious, and even contemplative, meaning of the worship of 'signs', and told us how 'idol-worship' had helped him to enter more deeply into the mystery of the signs used by the Church as means of grace and in order to 'concretize' the worship of God's people—especially that essential sign which constitutes the Church, the Eucharist.

A last speaker—for it is not possible to quote all—told us of the admiration aroused in him by the devotion of the Marathas. His studies had familiarized him with the great mystics of Mahārashtra, expecially Tukārām, the peasant who composed magnificent 'psalms' to the glory of his Lord. He described how following in Tukaram's footsteps and singing his 'gradual psalms,'* he had accompanied the crowds of pilgrims who come every year, sometimes from great distances, to the sanctuary of Viṭhobā at Pandhārpur. He too helped us to understand the religious value of *bhakti*, and to realize that the Lord conceals himself under the humblest of signs to meet his own and lead them to the very heart of the mystery in which he dwells.

So each one gave his own witness, concerning either *jñāna* (knowledge) or *bhakti* (devotion) or *karma* (service), each according to his particular gift and his personal vocation—each too according to the special circumstances in which providence had placed him.

Two conclusions stood out more and more clearly as the days passed. The first was that the Lord is already in India, and we need not imagine, poor feeble creatures that we are, that it is we who make him present. Our role is to help the holy seed which had already been sown by the Spirit in men's hearts and in their traditions to germinate—or better, to put ourselves at his service for the cultivation of this seed in the very soil in which he had planted it, and according to the conditions of development which he himself had laid down.

The second conclusion was that India had received from her Creator a very special gift of interiority and a unique inward orientation of the spirit. Therefore no presentation of the message of the Resurrection has any hope of awakening an echo in the spiritual heart of India, unless its own essential interiority shines forth in such a way as to penetrate to those secret depths in which the Lord had willed to hide his chosen children here in India. The presentation of the message is

---

*'gradual psalms'—an allusion to a group of psalms in the Bible (Pss. 120 ff) traditionally sung by Jewish pilgrims as they approached the holy city Jerusalem.

to be understood not merely as the direct preaching of the Gospel, but as the whole life of the Church which should be a perpetual revelation of that message—her rites, her institutions, her prayers, indeed, the whole way of life of the Christian people, and especially of those who are the leaders of that people.

Another quite unexpected result of this meeting was our discovery of each other as Christians. The original intention had been to bring together a group of exclusively Roman Catholic priests and theologians. However, the memory of the Shantivanam meetings led to the proposal that here also some non-Roman friends should be invited. No one objected, and so the wonder occurred.

All of us, Protestants and Catholics alike, had of course had previous contacts with members of other Christian confessions on the human and even the theological plane; but here, from the very outset, we passed beyond all such levels. The call of the Spirit to that inner depth of the self which is the grace and, as it seems, the special mission of India, heard and responded to together, led us to recognize each other as Christians at a hitherto unsuspected depth of inwardness and truth. We knew each other as brothers in Christ on a level at which all apparent differences were in a manner transcended. "It is like an *anamnesis** of the Church before the divisions," said one of the participants—"or a prophecy in the Spirit of unity restored," added another.

Each of us, however, preserved intact his own theological convictions and confessional loyalty. It was precisely as holding firmly to his own convictions and identified with his own particular denomination, that he expected to be recognized by his brethren as a sincere and authentic disciple of Christ. Yet each of us also felt very strongly that our deep commitment to Christ, even though manifested in forms which divide us from each other, is something far more important than all differences and even oppositions on the institutional and confessional level. It cannot be doubted that when all Christians and all groups of Christians now separated from each other, become aware of the depths in which

---

*Anamnesis—a Greek word which means 'memory', or rather 'memorial'. It is a remembering which actualizes and makes present what is remembered. Compare the use of the word in connection with the Eucharist, and its liturgical use for the part of the Canon which *recalls* the divine work of our redemption.

their faith in Christ is rooted—that dimension of interiority on which India insists so strongly—then the theological and institutional differences which keep us apart will appear in a totally new light, and it will become clear to the Church, thenceforth undivided in fact as well as in principle, how they may be resolved.

Thus, face to face with India, and by the grace of the Lord shining through India's religious thought and spiritual expeience, we Christians became more deeply conscious of our unity in that same Lord.

Rajpur

The following year we were the guests of the Christian Retreat and Study Centre at Rajpur, at the foot of the Himalayas on the road from Dehra Dun to Mussoorie. This time it was not the great chain of distant peaks that formed our horizon, but instead the lower slopes of the foothills, while to the south we looked down on the vast expanse of the Gangetic plain.

The choice of a place was of great importance for the success of our meetings. To enter fully into the spirit which should animate them, we needed above all complete isolation from the world, absence of noise, an atmosphere of peace and recollection, and a sufficient remoteness to discourage visitors who might lack the necessary preparation. All this Rajpur offered us, though in a completely different setting from that of Almora. Moreover—and this was an advantage we greatly appreciated—all the material arrangements were looked after by the management of the Centre.

The programme for Rajpur was more fully worked out than at Almora. We had decided to have a fixed time-table, and in the evening, whether we felt like it or not, we interrupted our after-dinner conversation to read the Bible and sing Compline. A definite theme had also been chosen for each session, taken from Hindu spirituality in the morning and from Christian spirituality in the evening. After a presentation, which took from twenty to thirty minutes, discussion and exchange of views began and sometimes continued without interruption for two hours at a stretch.

The previous meeting at Almora had served to put things into focus. The conclusion to which we were led was of the necessity for us as Christians to integrate into our own life of faith the dimension of interiority which is characterstic of the Hindu spiritual approach. This naturally led to the question: "Can Hindu interiority be taken over by

Christians just as it is?"

In the first place, Christianity is a historical religion; it is founded on events dated in time—the birth of Jesus under Caesar Augustus, his ministry in the time of Tiberius, his execution under the procurator Pontius Pilate. Can history be 'interiorized' without losing its essential connection with time? For the Hindu, history never has more than a symbolic value, and the 'incarnations' of Hindu mythology were not necessarily historical events at all.

Again Christianity is essentially an 'encounter' between man and a personal God. Can this encounter be interiorized without vanishing altogether into the a-personalism of Advaita?

Thirdly, Christian experience is based on man's recognition of his sinfulness, and begins with repentance. But in the absolute interiority proclaimed by Hinduism there is no place for real sin, and therefore none for true repentance.

Stated in these terms as it so frequently is, the problem is insoluble. The questions with which Hindu experience, by the very fact of its existence, confronts Christianity compel the Christian to rethink the philosophical principles on which he has based his theology. His concepts especially of time and creation, of personality and encounter, need to be examined afresh and deepened in the light of Eastern experience. There is here no question of replacing Western concepts with Eastern ones, but rather of trying to enter more deeply into both, in order first of all to discover in each case wthat is the solid ground of the experience known by intuition, and then to work out a way of expressing that experience which will be valid, even if inevitably it is not the only one possible.

The first Hindu teacher whose spiritual approach was presented to us was Shankara, the supreme master of Advaita. For him the ultimate spiritual experience is that of the Self, the One-without-a-second, the Ātman which is identical with Brahman. This supreme Reality cannot be adequately represented by any concept. The ascent to the Real is by way of pure negation—"*neti, neti*", "not this, not this"—the negation of all that passes away, all that is only appearance, and which therefore cannot be the Real in itself. In the Real there is neither duality nor difference. The supreme experience is of pure non-duality, and there alone truth is found.

The created world is neither real nor unreal. It is *maya*, as lacking in stability as the pictures which flit across a cine screen. It has no significance except on its own level and for anyone who has not yet discovered the level of the Real, namely himself in his essential truth.

The truth of Being is known only by revelation (the Scriptures) or by experience. Reason cannot bring one to it, still less works, either ritual or any other. The Self shines in its own splendour. The experience of the Self simply *is*. No road leads to it, and none ever reaches it. All that a man can do is it free himself by following the way of renunciation and of negating all the 'illusory' attributes super-imposed on the Real itself—which he himself simply *is*.

Another example of pure Advaita is Ramaṇa Maharshi, the sage of Arunāchala (or Tiruvannāmalai) who died in 1950. He had no philosophical training and, at the outset, had not even read the Scriptures. Only several years after the experience which transformed his life did he discover that this experience was precisely that which is described in the holy books and the writings of the learned. There was moreover nothing in his psychological make-up to suggest that his experience could be explained in terms of the spontaneous eruption of a highly charged subconscious. What happened to him was that one day, at the age of seventeen, he had a sudden conviction that he was going to die. With full awareness of what he was doing, he decided to accept the experience of dying, which so closely resembles falling asleep. Everything faded away from his mind, and soon even from his consciousness, apart from an essential awareness concentrated on one central and unique point, that "I am". Every attribute of that "I am" had disappeared. Nothing was left except the sheer awareness of being in its crystal purity and unbounded fullness.

Can this experience that *I am*, the essential experience of Vedānta, be integrated into Christianity?

Some one has said: "The Christian experience is, or at least starts from, the confession that *I am not* (the nothingness of the creature, the less-than-nothingness of the sinner)." But is such an affirmation of not-being in fact possible? *Who* is saying "I am not"?

The experience that *I am* is truly the fundamental experience of each conscious being, that which controls all the rest. That was why Srī Ramaṇa centred all his spiritual guidance and teaching on the simple question: "Who am I?" "Who are you? Find out who you really are, and the rest will inevitably follow."

The Christian appropriation of the Maharshi's teaching must be sought along another line, in the depths of the inner silence where, beyond all words, even the word *I*, the experience of being, is disclosed. For him whose inner ear is attuned to the murmur of the Spirit, this silence resounds with the voice of the Father who utters himself in his Son, and in that Son calls into being all that exists: "Thou art my Son"—the primordial *Thou* answering to the essential *I* of Being.

The Bhagavad-Gītā reflects all the fundamental tendencies of Indian spirituality—so much so that teachers of the stature of Shankara or Rāmānuja could write commentaries on it which practically contradict each other.

The advaitic experience is rather rare, at least in its fullest form. It was therefore necessary to provide for the ordinary believer a spiritual path more within his reach, and accordingly the Gita seeks to lead the religious man in the way of love and devotion. It also wisely takes account of the fact that to aim at total non-activity is to pursue a chimera, a Utopian dream. What is needed therefore is to do all that we have to do—the performance of ritual acts and all the other duties required by daily life or by circumstances—simply because it is commanded by the Scriptures, out of disinterested love for the Lord alone, without looking for any personal advantage whatever. This, according to the Gita, is the surest way of achieving liberation and passing to the Lord at the hour of death.

It is often said that the Gita is the book which more than any other contains the richness and real depth of the Hindu spiritual tradition. Certainly it is the most widely-read book in India. But it cannot be rightly understood if it is isolated from that tradition as a whole, and even more so, if certain passages or single verses which appear more obviously intelligible are taken by themselves.

It is also said that the Hinduism of the Gita can be more easily 'Christianized' than that of the Upanishads. No doubt its insistence on love, loving surrender to the Lord and disinterested action seems familiar to the Christian reader. But it must not be forgotten that even in the Gita the personality of the Lord is perilously insubstantial; moreover, traces of a latent pantheism are constantly in evidence, and disinterested action as here understood would exclude even the desire for final beatitude. In short, the way of love and works advocated by the Gita, no less than the radical advaita of Shankara or Ramaṇa Maharshi, requires a wholesale renewal and transformation from within before it can become a genuinely Christian 'way of salvation'.

On the last morning we were invited to reflect upon the spirituality of Śrī Aurobindo. His distinctive intuition was that in the supreme experience the *manifold* cannot be separated from the *one*, and that humanity is on the move towards an era of awareness in which the divine, in the form of the 'supra–mental', will invade the world of the manifold. Aurobindo will have nothing to do with the ruthless renunciations and negations of the strictly advaitic path; the being of man in its entirety, including his body, must be assumed by the divine through an ascesis which Śrī Aurobindo calls 'integral yoga'.

Some people may be disconcerted by the conceptual imagery in which these intuitions are expressed. However, no attempt at a 'Christian transcendence' of Advaita can afford to neglect the thought of Śrī Aurobindo, any more than it can neglect Rāmānuja, for whom the advaitic experience as formulated by Shankara remains only a stage on the way to the supreme experience.

The first Christian master of spirituality to be studied was Meister Eckhart, who could be regarded as a parallel to Shankara. He also sought to attain to the mystery of God in the depths of the self by following a path of negation and total nakedness, refusing to make use of concepts or feelings or any kind of support from within or without. For him, nothing but God could be an image of God; nothing but God could be the way to God.

Once it has arrived at this perfect purity, the soul discovers the purity of her own essence within the very mystery of God. She can no longer distinguish herself from God. Hence arose the paradoxes in the Master's teaching which led to his trial and condemnation—a trial which, one cannot help feeling, might well have had a different outcome, if it has been conducted in an atmosphere less charged with human passion and by persons with a less academic understanding of theology.

At times indeed Eckhart seems to imply that the 'Godhead' in some way transcends the divine Persons. In this he was a victim of Latin Trinitarian theology, which took the divine nature as its starting point and then proceeded to the Persons. Such a theology was incapable of expressing what he had experienced of the 'deep things of God'. What fundamentally attracted him was the mystery of the Father as the ultimate source of the Trinity, 'before' (to use an impossible expression) the Son was born of him—the divine mystery in the *śūnya* which has so fascinated Buddhist contemplatives—God *before* he is anything that can be named, neither Father, nor Son nor Spirit; the unmanifested God before he can even be called God. It was here, in the mystery of the unmanifested and the wholly ineffable, that Eckhart discovered also his own pure essence 'before' he existed at all. He was not the only man of his period to experience this particular kind of fascination. One will only be tempted to dismiss it as kind of intellectual game, if one has never been drawn by the Spirit into the mysterious regions which lie beyond all the ready-made definitions and 'clear and distinct ideas' which men employ to think about God.

After Eckhart we discussed the spirituality of the Eastern Christians which is so much closer to the heart of India than that of the Latin Church. If Russian monks had evangelized India, they would not have needed any of the complicated and far too rationalistic 'adaptations' which Western Christians often feel obliged to adopt. The witness of a Russian monk, in word and life, would have immediate effect.

Hesychasm, for instance, and the 'Jesus Prayer' which goes with it, embody methods of spiritual discipline and contemplation which are perfectly familiar in India. The Jesus Prayer had its counterpart in *nāma-japa*, the continual repetition of the name of the Lord. Hesychasm, like Yoga, makes use of certain bodily postures and ways of breathing to promote recollection.

The Jesus Prayer, at first uttered with the lips and tongue, should gradually become more and more interior, invading the mind and finally taking up its abode in the heart. Then only the soul is established in God, and no place is henceforth left for any evil thought, for the Prayer has taken complete possession. Only one who has experienced it can describe this peaceful penetration of the Name of Jesus into the heart.

From another angle, the three stages of this ascent may be described as contemplation of nature, contemplation of the Scriptures, and entry into the mystery of God. This entry is the summit of the spiritual life, the coming of the Holy Spirit, for which we ask every day in the Lords's Prayer, when we say, "Thy Kingdom come." Simeon the New Theologian and, closer to our time Seraphim of Sarov, have left us unforgettable accounts of this final possession by the Spirit.

This experience, however, could never be expressed in the non-dualist terms of Vedānta or Master Eckhart; for in the same instant the soul becomes so intensely aware of herself as nothingness and sin, that her invocation of Christ as the Son of the living God ends almost inevitably with "Have mercy on me, a sinner." Moreover, this experience is not confined to the individual who has it; he draws into it the whole Church, and indeed the entire universe, in the communion of the Spirit.

Gregory of Nyssa offers the rare spectacle of theologian who fearlessly set himself to study the writings of 'pagan' philosophers. This made it possible for him to express his own Christian experience with unusual felicity in categories borrowed from Plato and Plotinus.

For Plotinus the *nous*, man's intelligence, was divine. Gregory, in the light of Genesis, sees it more accurately as the image of God in man. The whole of man's spiritual life consists in the striving of this image to be reunited with its archetype. Indeed, it is in this stretching out, *epektasis*, that man attains to God. "One cannot know God except in one's inability to know him." "The desire for God is itself the vision of God." The Christian life is an unending ascent, an unquenchable aspiration towards the divine essence which ever remains hidden, for even in the life to come the *epektasis* will continue without ceasing through an eternity of aeons. At last the soul surrenders itself to God and, having thus left behind all that she had and attained to being, she possesses him in renouncing all possession, in the ecstasy of pure love.

The contemplation of Gregory of Nyssa, like that of Hesychasm in later centuries, is Christ-centred, ecclesial and cosmic. A spirituality based on the notion of the *image* of God could not have been anything else.

In the final session at Rajpur a parallel was drawn between John of the Cross and Shankara on the one hand, and Teresa of Avila and Rāmānuja on the other.

In John of the Cross we find essentially the same approach as that of Shankara, without of course his philosophical substructure. Apophatism, detachment, negation—these the master of the *Ascent of Mount Carmel* and of the *Dark Night* preaches unremittingly. Only in the *nothing* is to be found the *all*. Like Shankara he invites us to penetrate to the 'deepest centre' beyond all the superficial levels of the soul. However, in this deepest centre of his heart it is not a cold and impersonal Absolute that he finds, but the superabundant life of the Blessed Trinity, in which the transformed spirit of man is invited to share...

As for St Teresa, she—like Rāmānuja—is more drawn to the way of devotion. She knows that the Lord lives and abides within her. All her desire is simply to rest her head, like Magdalene, against his sacred feet.

We parted from each other with the determination to continue next year our research on the vital question of how to integrate Hindu interiority with Christian spirituality. Many problems had been raised during our meeting. Before they could be solved, they needed to mature in our minds and be pondered in our prayers.

3
RETURN TO THE SOURCES

HOWEVER in the course of subsequent correspondence and individual encounters we gradually came to ask whether we should not change the plan of action followed in the two first meetings.

The non-Roman members of the group, particularly the Presbyterians, were unanimous in their recognition of the exceptional interest of our discussion, and even said that they envied the depth at which this search for dialogue between India and the Church was being carried on. Moreover, 'the *anamnesis* of the undivided Church' had been experienced as strongly at Rajpur as at Almora, especially by those who had there joined us for the first time. Nevertheless a certain regret made itself felt among them. Should not our study be centred more directly and more explicitly upon the Word of God? At Rajpur indeed we had read a chapter of the Bible each evening before Compline, and at the beginning of each session a passage from Scripture had been suggested for all to meditate on in silence, as a Biblical and spiritual introduction to the theme which was to be developed afterwards. But they would have liked something more. Would it not be possible to set aside a definite time each day for common study and meditation on the Scriptures, as is the regular practice in gatherings of Evangelical Christians?

This suggestion was accepted. Then one day, in the middle of a conversation, someone suddenly had an inspiration: "Why should we not read the Upanishads in the same way?" Strange as this idea appeared at first sight, we realized as we thought about it that it was full of possibilities and deserved at least a serious trial. Thus we tentatively decided upon the plan which was actually followed at Nagpur—to have meditative reading in common of the Bible in the morning and of the Upanishads in the evening.

In the meantime, some members of the group who happened to be in Delhi decided to meet at the home of one of their number, the (Anglican) Brotherhood of the Ascended Christ, for what they called a 'probe' (this was at the time when the Russians and Americans were competing with each other in sending 'probes' or 'soundings' into space). The experiment was fully justified. On the last evening the then Coadjutor-Archbishop of Delhi accepted an invitation to join the party; and on the following day he confided to one of them what a revelation this prayerful and ecclesial reading of the Upanishads had been for him, first of all, of the interiority of the Hindu Scriptures which he had not previously suspected; and secondly of the challenge offered to the Church, and especially to her ministers, by the existence in India of such a profoundly contemplative spirit.

A new circular was then sent to the members of the group, giving the reasons for the change of programme and explaining the methods that we would be using, so that each might prepare himself adequately and maintain a common approach. As the letter pointed out, the change was only apparent. We had already decided to study the return to the sources which contact with Hindu spirituality makes essential for Christians. The contemplative and ecclesial reading of Biblical and Hindu texts now suggested would compel each of us to experience this return in an existential way, suited to his own spiritual life.

Hindu mystical tradition bears witness to the existence of levels of spiritual awareness which are too often neglected by Christians. It is true that the Hindu experience of interiority takes place rather at the pancosmic or metacosmic level, and rarely attains to the personal, or rather interpersonal, dimension of Being revealed by God to men in the Hebrew and Christian Scriptures. But our Christian meditation on the Upanishads would directly contribute to awakening and at the same time redeeming in us these profound levels or dimensions of the Hindu experience. It would be for them a kind of baptism and final illumination, a resurrection and eschatological fulfilment. Indeed, we would thus be contemplating the Lord Christ, the goal of the cosmos, through Hindu eyes, and so 'redeeming' the essential values of the Hindu tradition which are in danger of being swept away in the current of contemporary materialism.

The Bible

In spite of the term 'Bible Study', which we adopted because it had been hallowed by long use, our reading of the Bible was not to consist in speculative or exegetical analysis of the text. We envisaged rather a prayerful reading, the *lectio divina* of Patristic and monastic tradition, a reading done in the Presence and aiming above all at inward assimilation of the message of God under the guidance of his Spirit.

Moreover, this reading was to be undertaken within the community (*koinonia*) of the Church—that Church of which every group of believers gathered together in the name of the Lord is already the sign (Matt. 18:20), and whose unity is shown sacramentally in the 'breaking of bread' celebrated in common (Acts 2:42).

This would involve the quietening of our understanding and having what the Bible calls a 'listening heart'; even more it demands the silence of our instinctive egotism which urges us to impose our own views, our own aims, our own impressions, even in the holiest matters, and so often drowns the voice of the Spirit. It would also mean that we must allow ourselves to be 'vulnerable' to the Word of God, and to the unpredictable demands with which he is liable to confront us when we come face to face with him in the holy Scriptures. Faced with the living actuality of the Word of God in the Bible, man can only tremble; but relying on his faith, the Christian should remain steadfastly open to his call.

Lastly, as the foundation of all this, we must have a firm purpose of *metanoia* or conversion. Otherwise we should not be ready to change, to 'turn back' (*con-versio*), if God should require it of us, to 'obey the Gospel', as Paul puts it in his Epistle to the Romans (10:16).

It was therefore proposed that, after a moment of recollection and a prayer drawn from Christian tradition, the Scriptural passage should be read in two different translations, followed by a brief commentary by one of the group, aimed at bringing out its essential points. The chief purpose of this commentary would be to show the relevance of the message for those who were listening to it at that moment, Christians of India, or at least Christians involved in the mission of the Church in India, called to serve India in her approach to the Church, and the Church in her advance to meet India. The commentator should be far less eager to propound his own pet ideas than to help his brother to enter more deeply into the thought of the inspired author and become more fully open to the action of the Spirit present in the Word.

There would follow ten or fifteen minutes of recollection, to be spent in either reflecting on the text in the presence of the Master within, or simply waiting on him in silence.

After this would begin the sharing of the thoughts and questions awakened in each one during his hearing of and meditation on the sacred Word.

It was insisted that the most important thing of all was to preserve the contemplative character of this reading within the fellowship of the Church. Careful theological and exegetical preparation was certainly not excluded, but it was assumed that this would be done in advance. The statement of differences of opinion that might arise was not ruled out, nor was frank and fraternal discussion of apparently conflicting points of view. But the basic attitude necessary for each one in order to make this free exchange possible would be that of seeking in the fellowship of the Church to listen to and question the Spirit in his brothers, and in turn to pass on to them whatever he thought in the Spirit ought to be passed on.

The Upanishads

The reading of the Upanishads was to follow the same pattern as that of the Bible. Based on the same principles and carried out in the same way. it too would be contemplative, always within the fellowship of the Church, and marked by the same openness to the spirit, each one listening and asking questions, humbly making suggestions and never dogmatically laying down the law.

The programme adopted at Nagpur consisted of a moment of recollection followed by the 'hymn of peace' from the Iśa Upanishad (*pūrṇam adaḥ....,* see chapter 5); next a Sanskrit litany to Jesus, the Lord, the anointed One, the Saviour, the Son of Man, the God-Man; then a verse from the Purāṇas affirming the supremacy of the Lord; and finally, the singing of the well-known verse of the Brihadāraṇyaka Upanishad:

> From non-being lead me to Being;
> from darkness lead me to light;
> from death lead me to immortality.

This was to be followed by the reading of the Upanishad in two versions, its chanting in Sanskrit, a brief commentary, fifteen minutes of silence, and the fraternal exchange of reflections.

The circular letter especially warned against the temptation to institute a premature comparison between Biblical and Sanskrit texts, leading to hasty judgments about the latter in the light of the former. It insisted strongly on the point that we were coming together above all to *listen* to what the Hindu Scriptures mysteriously foreshadowed of Christ in that 'attitude of listening' so warmly recommended by Pope Paul VI in his encyclical *Ecclesiam Suam.** This presupposes first of all, with

---

*"Before speaking ourselves, we must first listen with great attention to the other man's words, and even more to his heart."

the Upanishad no less than with the Bible, a very humble approach to the literal sense; our first task is to understand in the Upanishad what a Hindu (not a pure exegete, nor a pure philosopher, but a spiritual Hindu who is open both to personal experience and to living tradition) himself understands by it. The Christian interpretation of the Upanishads must issue from the authentically Hindu understanding of them in their entirety, in the same way as the topmost branches of a tree reach up towards the sky only because they are supported by the trunk, solidly rooted in the earth. To single out individual texts, which seem to have more in common with Christian ideas or even with the Western mental outlook, and then indulge in 'Christian' speculation based upon them, would be to betray both Hinduism and Christianity.

The primary object of the Christian reading of the Upanishads in the presence of Christ was, as has already been said, to rediscover in ourselves the 'secret place' experienced by the rishis, and then, under the guidance of the Spirit, in an existential process wholly personal to each one, to allow the Christian expression and Trinitarian consummation of this experience to find its full development in us. In the Bible itself the revelation of Christ was only gradual. "Before Abraham was, I am," declared Jesus. But who knew him then? The revelation of the mystery of God was accomplished by progressive 'unveilings'. It began with Adam and will be completed only at the end of time. What the Christian finds in the Upanishads, if he reads them attentively, is precisely an unveiling of this mystery which takes place according to the measure of his own growth in sensitivity to the inner 'voice'. The mystery of Christ is not clearly revealed in the Upanishads, any more than it was in the Old Testament. Moreover, the insights expressed in them do not bear upon the same aspects of the mystery as those glimpsed by the prophets and sages of Israel. St Paul boldly says that he no longer regards Christ 'according to the flesh,' from a human point of view. St John, for his part, constantly invites us to contemplate the eternal mystery of Christ and his oneness with the Father in the Spirit. It would seem that it is into this interior and transcendent aspect of the mystery of Jesus that the Upanishads should help us to enter.

Some would have preferred to have had the reading of the Upanishads in the morning, making it a kind of preparation for the Bible reading, as Advent precedes Christmas. If the Bible was then read in the evening, it would be heard as the crowning and perfecting by the Word of God of all that men taught by the Spirit have sensed or conceived of him. For the Spirit leads us to the Son, as the Son does to the Father. In the end, however, we kept to the order originally planned; and as it turned out, the evening readings from the Upanishads heard in the light of the previous Bible pasages, somehow found their fulfilment and completion in the Bible readings of the following day. It often happened that successive passages from the Bible and the Upanishads linked up with and illuminated each other in a wonderful way, without any deliberate planning of this on our part. It was like a continual progress into the 'deep places' of the soul. "They go from strength to strength ; the God of gods will be seen (by them) in Zion" (Ps.84:7), and "deep calls to deep" (Ps.42:7).

It was, moreover, fitting that the Bible should come first, for the Christian approaches the Upanishads already enriched by his faith, his personal experience in Christ and his sensitivity to the Spirit. It is precisely his practice of reading the holy Scriptures and recognizing the inspiration of the Spirit in the writings of prophets and apostles—not to mention some of the more unlikely pages in the history of Israel—that has made him capable of recognizing the voice of God in everything. That Voice indeed sounds throughout the universe and the whole of time, as it fills the heart of man, making itself heard throughout the evolution of the cosmos and the unfolding of human history, and even more mysteriously through the words of certain privileged spirits describing their own intimate knowledge of God—those whom Thomas Aquinas, echoing Dionysius the Areopagite, describes as *'non solum discentes, sed patientes divina'*—'not merely learning about, but experiencing God.'

Certainly, if a Christian wants his study of the Upanishads to be worth anything, he must temporarily put on one side, *en epoché*,* not indeed his Christian faith, but at least to a great extent the conceptual expression of that faith. It is even more necessary for him to try to free himself from his personal and sociological conditioning. He must see that he does not allow the concepts in which dogma or theology have as it were encased the revelation to invade his mind while he is reading and set up a continual opposition to the concepts through which the Upanishadic experience is transmitted to him. Rather he must first of all listen to the witness of this experience itself, trying to make himself totally transparent to it, to assimilate himself to it as deeply as possible. Above all, he must see that he does not shut out the echoes and overtones which this message will sometimes awaken in his heart. He is

---

*See note on page 12.

not reading the Upanishads as part of a course in comparative religion, but in order to enter as authentically as possible into the experience which has moulded the religious soul of India. How else could the treasures of this experience ever be gathered into the storehouse of the Church? How else could this precious seed, providentially safeguarded by the Spirit, germinate in Christian souls, no less providentially prepared to receive it, so as to "bring forth fruit a hundredfold" in the words of the parable (Mark 4:8)? It is Israel's privilege to "suck the breast of kings" in Isaiah's vigorous phrase; but how else can one be nourished by this milk, except by clinging to the breast from which it flows?

It goes without saying that this attitude of mind does not in any way endanger the Christian's underlying disposition of faith, openness to the Spirit and self-transcendence in the depth of his being. Indeed, the attitude of deep faith which makes a Christian what he is, contains within itself all the essentials of the advaitic experience; for it is always and everywhere in his faith in the revealed Word that the Christian hears and listens to the Spirit.

If this principle of *epoché* was accepted in advance by the whole group, it would allow complete freedom in discussion and the exchange of views. It would be understood that anyone could freely ask any question or express any reaction suggested to him by the reading of the Hindu texts, secure in the knowledge that he was among fully committed Christian brothers who all recognized each other as such. No one would dream of doubting another's faith on the ground of forms of expression, which might still be groping and imprecise, too much influenced by Vedantic terminology to correspond to the exact but conceptually very limited formulations of traditional theology. We would be able to think aloud together and submit to each other for consideration ideas which might seem to be overbold, the first uncertain steps of men emerging from the night of the advaitic experience.

Such were the preparations for the meeting which took place at Nagpur between Christmas 1963 and Epiphany 1964. Nagpur was finally chosen because of its central position. The Himalayas had certainly provided a magnificent and inspiring setting, but the fatigue of the long journey weighed heavily on those who had to travel from the south of India. The accommodaion which was kindly offered to us by the General Secretary of the National Christian Council of India, was very pleasant, sufficiently far from the noise and bustle of the city, and surrounded by a large garden which looked out over lovely country.

As on former occasions, the day began with the Eucharistic sacrifice. This was usually a Latin Mass sung to Gregorian chant, but we also had celebrations in the Chaldean rite of Malabar in Malayalam and in the Syro-Malankara rite in English. Unfortunately, the non-Roman brethren had once again to meet separately to celebrate the liturgy before coming to unite themselves, by prayer and song, to our community offering. In the evening Compline, sung according to the ancient English rite of Sarum, brought us together once more in adoration and thanksgiving.

This time the meeting lasted for a whole week, from Saturday evening to midday of the following Saturday. The Archbishop of Nagpur, Mgr Eugene D'Souza (since translated to the newly created see of Bhopal) was present at most of our meetings. He had just returned from the second session of the Vatican Council, at which he had made several courageous interventions. He gave us the warmest encouragement and, like the practical man he is, suggested several ways of increasing the influence of our group. The Principal of Hislop College, Nagpur, Dr D.G. Moses, a President of the World Council of Churches, also attended our conference as often as he could. Another very welcome visitor was the Anglican Bishop of Nagpur, J.W. Sadiq, himself recently returned from Rome where he had been an observer at the Council.

The discussions were very free and devoid of all formality. We met regularly in the garden, seated cross-legged in a circle under a great tree, only changing our position when necessary to avoid the sun.

4
THE GENTILES IN THE BIBLE

THE Biblical texts for the morning sessions were chosen to help us to understand in the light of the Word of God what is meant by 'the manifestation of the Spirit' (1Cor. 12:7) in a non-Christian culture.

When the Old Testament refers to 'the nations' it certainly uses at times language of extreme harshness. They seem to be simply doomed to slaughter and extermination on the 'great day' of Yahweh's wrath, or at best to perpetual slavery within the restored kingdom of Israel. However, it is not difficult to find here and there in the Bible other texts which have a very different ring. It is especially to these texts that the Spirit seems to be drawing the attention of Christians today, when the Church finds herself with a certain astonishment in the midst of an *oikoumené*, a known and inhabited world which now extends to the remotest corners of the earth.

It is surely very significant that one of the most remarkable books in the Old Testament bears the name of Job, a dweller in the land of Uz, one who is therefore not a Jew; and that this 'pagan' was given by God to his own people as a model of patience. Again, when Ezekiel wants to name three righteous men who might possibly be able to check the divine anger, as once Abraham had interceded with God for Sodom (Gen. 18:22ff), where does he find them? First there is Noah, who can be regarded as a remote ancestor of the chosen people; but with him the prophet associates this same 'man of Uz', Job the Arab sheikh, and the mysterious figure of Danel, a Canaanite king whose reputation for wisdom was still a living tradition in Palestine (Ez. 14:14). Then the master-craftsman who was chosen to cast the pillars and the sea of bronze and to fashion the vessels and other utensils destined for the service of Yahweh in Solomon's temple, was in fact a resident alien, one Huram Abi, son of a man of Tyre (2 Chron. 2:13; 4:16) Nor should we forget that the Lord willed to include in his human genealogy not merely righteous men and women but also prostitutes, not only Jews but also Ruth the Moabitess and Rahab the

Canaanite. Some may be tempted to say that these are very insignificant pointers, yet can we dare to set limits to the mystery contained in the word of God?

Gentile priests

The first Bible passages proposed for our meditation were those which speak of Melchizedek, whose memory the Holy Father was just then recalling in his homily at Bethlehem. Melchizedek is mentioned in Genesis (ch.14), in the Psalms (Ps.110), and in the Epistle to the Hebrews (ch.7). He was at the same time both king and priest, king of Salem and priest of the enigmatic El Elyon, a title explained by the translators of the Septuagint as 'the Most High God'. Abraham bowed before him to receive his blessing and offered him the tribute of a tithe of the spoil. In the person of Abraham all the holy people of Israel and the whole Aaronic priesthood bowed before the priest of the cosmic Covenant and offered the tithe as a token of their subordination (Heb. 7:7-10). Later on it was revealed to the Psalmist that it was "according to the order of Melchizedek" that the Messiah himself would be a priest—"a priest for ever". The author of the Epistle to the Hebrews saw Melchizedek as an antitype of the Son of God; while the Roman Canon recalls the memory of Melchizedek and asks that the offering of the people of God may be as acceptable to him as that of the priest who blessed Abraham.

But who, after all, was Melchizedek if not a Canaanite priest of the 'cosmic religion'? He exercised his priesthood independently of any mission received from the *debar Yahweh*, the word of the Lord. He worshipped according to the traditional rites of his own people, and had never been granted any revelation like that given to Abraham. He was not so different from those contemporary Vedic priests—rather he might be called their brother—who were even then offering sacrifice to God according to their own traditions among the Himalayan peaks or on the Gangetic plains; or even from their successors by natural descent or ritual intiation who to this day continue to adore God under the name of Shiva the Beneficent at the foot of Kedarnath or at Arunachala, the flame-crowned mountain of the Dravidian countryside.

Of course it is always possible for exegetes to minimize the significance of these passage. But this does not alter the fact that it can hardly have been without the connivance of the Holy Spirit that this stray text, which cannot be attributed to any of the known sources of the Pentateuch, was included in Genesis and that the figure of Melchizedek exercised such a remarkable fascination upon the Psalmist, the author of Hebrews and the first generations of Christians.

According to the Bible itself, then, we have to go behind the Mosaic priesthood and liturgy to the priestly cult of the cosmic religion, in order to find the first foreshadowing of the unique sacrifice of the Saviour and the liturgy of the New Covenant. It is precisely in view of its eschatological fulfilment in the Church that this cosmic liturgy is already pleasing to God, "a holy sacrifice, a spotless victim", as it is boldly called in the Roman canon.

This surely means that we are invited, whenever we are present at any religious ceremony in India, to open wide our minds and hearts to discern, beyond the vivid sights and sounds which meet our senses, the very reality which these liturgies mysteriously foreshadow. If we find certain aspects of them difficult to integrate into this perspective, we should perhaps remind ourselves what the Jewish cult was really like and how at the great festivals the temple was transformed into a slaughterhouse. Nor can we forget certain of the prayers in the Psalms which the Church still places on our lips, despite the reluctance of our Chriystian hearts to utter them.

The parallel text of Malachi (1:11) was not studied in detail at Nagpur, as it had been discussed at Delhi a few months earlier. The ultimately Eucharistic reference of this prophetic text was certainly ratified by the Council of Trent. But this is no more than a further proof that the mystery which finds its eschatological fulfilment in Christ is present in Gentile worship under the form of prophecy and sign. There can be no doubt that the prophet actually had in mind the offerings which were daily presented to the Lord Most High, the God of heaven, from furthest east to furthest west of the Persian Empire, to which Palestine at that time belonged.

The offering of the heart is of far greater value in the sight of God than any ritual sacrifice, which can never be more than a sign. But wherever an offering is made to the Lord from a sincere and truly devoted heart, it surely foreshadows the redemptive sacrifice of the Lamb, made ready from the beginning of time, and finally manifested in the paschal mystery.

The Treasures of the Nations

The second day's Bible study was devoted to Isaiah, c. with which were associated some parallel texts from the same prop. and also the verses from Chapter 21 of Revelation which echo them so strikingly. It must certainly be admitted that some of the verses in this chapter clearly envisage the nations and their kings coming up to Jerusalem as slaves, bowed beneath the yoke and henceforth destined to serve Yahweh and his people simply in virtue of being conquered, like the Canaanites who escaped destruction when Israel took possession of the Promised Land (Josh.9):

> Foreigners will rebuild your walls
> and their kings will be your servants...
> The sons of your oppressors will come to you bowing,
> at your feet shall fall all who despised you (Is. 60:10,14).

But that is by no means the whole story. First of all, we learn that the nations will come voluntarily to worship God in Zion and to learn his law (Isaiah 2:3), and that the sons of strangers will be welcomed into Yahweh's house of prayer and their offering will be accepted on his altar (56:7 ; cp. also 19:21, 24-25 and 18:7).

Even this is not all. In those days the wealth of the nations will be brought to Yahweh, to his temple and his people. It will become part of his treasure and will manifest his glory:

> All the flocks of Kedar will be gathered to you ....
> they will come up with acceptance on my altar,
> to adorn the Temple of my glory.
> The glory of Lebanon will come to you ...
> to beautify the place of my sanctuary,
> to glorify the resting place of my feet.
> You will be suckled on the milk of nations,
> suckled at the breast of kings (Is. 60:7,13,16).

Such texts, and similar passages elsewhere in Scripture, clearly show that the Church is destined to *receive* from the nations, and to receive not only material but also spiritual goods. Certainly no one would dare to limit to the material order the glorious enrichment which the Gentiles are to bring with them into the new Israel. Those whom the Church by baptism incorporates into herself and unites to the pleroma of the risen Lord are not mere anonymous bodies and souls, but *persons* individually called and 'named' by God. They have each been prepared by him with divine solicitude for this day, and when they enter the Church, they bring with them all the cultural and spiritual wealth that they have amassed—

> to adorn the Temple of his glory....
> to glorify the resting place of his feet.

Moses himself, after all, was providentially brought up at the court of Pharaoh and instructed in all the learning of the Egyptians, so that when the time came he could use it for the benefit of his people, the 'people of God'.

In conclusion, this passage contains an image of unequalled boldness and power, to which reference has already been made:

> You will be suckled on the milk of nations,
> suckled at the breast of kings (Is. 60:16);

One is not suckled at the breasts of an enemy or a slave—it is to a mother's breast that one clings—

> to be suckled, filled....
> to savour with delight her glorious breasts (Is. 66:11—JB);

and thus one receives from her that food sacred above all other which a mother prepares from her own substance to nourish her babe. It is impossible to imagine a more forceful way of expressing what the Lord has prepared in the very heart of the nations for his new people of Israel.

"Everything that was written about him"

Tuesday morning was devoted to those passages of the Gospel in which Jesus makes his disciples realize that the sacred texts of the Old Testament were 'written of him'. The most striking of these passages is in St Luke (24:44—JB). "Then he told them: This is what I meant when I said, while I was still with you, that everything written about me in the Law of Moses, in the Prophets and in the Psalms, has to be fulfilled."

Elsewhere in the Gospels we find many such references to Scripture: "This was done to fulfil what was written in...." For example, in John 19:28, "Jesus, knowing that all was now finished, said (to fulfil the scripture), 'I thirst'." And in 19:36 "These things took place that the scripture might be fulfilled ..."

It is certain that Jesus, as man, read in the Scriptures the detail of his Father's will for him, the way chosen by the Father for him to carry out his redemptive mission. For instance, he meditated on the Psalms. He quoted a Psalm when calling on the scribes to recognise him (Ps. 110:1 in Matt. 22:43-45). Again, on the cross he applied Ps. 22 to himself: "My God, my God, why have you forsaken me?" and also Ps. 31: "Into your hands I commend my spirit" (Mark 15:34; Luke 23:46). He had also pondered the writings of the prophets, and saw himself in Isaiah's 'Servant of Yahweh' and Daniel's 'Son of Man'. Throughout his life it was his concern to fulfil all that was foretold about him and expected of him.

It was not only in the Scriptures of his people that he discovered his Father's will for him. He found it in all the circumstances of his incarnation in time, in his cultural, racial and family background, in everything that 'defined' him in space and time, all that 'concretized' him as a man, as *this* man. All this was for him an expression of the will of God. Thus he was an obedient son to Joseph and Mary and, as he grew up, a faithful Jew, though no formalist, making no attempt to escape from the obeligations of his human birth on the grounds of his mysterious origin (Matt. 17:24ff; cp. Phil. 2:5ff). Jesus simply carried out his Father's will as he read it day by day, hour by hour, moment by moment, in the great book of the world and of human history, made up for him as for other men by the seemingly insignificant events of his ordinary life. Also in the historical and religious circumstances of his incarnate life, including the spiritual dispositions of the leaders of his people, Jesus as man discerned the way he must follow to carry out his redemptive work.

But it was above all in the religious traditions of his people, all oriented towards himself, and in the Scriptures in which everything written was written of him, that he found the clearest and most precise indications of his Father's will.

During the discussion someone objected that the Lord could not be bound, even by the Scriptures. He is himself the Lord of the Scriptures. If he offered himself to the Father in the Paschal Sacrifice, he did so 'of his own accord' (John 10:18), because of the love which blazed in the depth of his heart both for God his Father and for his human brothers.

There is surely no real opposition here. Neither the creation of the universe nor the historical circumstances of the Incarnation can be considered in isolation from the Paschal mystery to which the whole course of human history is directed and which is according to the divine plan the ultimate reason for everything. If the history of mankind and the conditions in which God became incarnate were such as they were, this was because Jesus, for whose sake they existed, had also to be such as he was, because the love which is identical with the very being of the Father could not be adequately revealed in any other way to man living in time. We can say, then, that Jesus as man read in the Scripture what he himself had, as God, written in them 'before the foundation of the world'.

In the Church the Lord continues his work of gathering up all the life and toil of succeeding generations into his unique and definitive Passover, his 'passing from this world to the Father'; she is therefore, the extension to all times and places of the incarnation of the Son of God, which actually took place as a historical fact in one determinate place and time.

It naturally follows from this that the Church, like her Lord in the days of his earthly life, is called to discern the Father's will for her in all the historical, social and cultural circumstances in which she actually finds herself. It is through the men in whom she is now embodied, through their traditions, mentality and language, that each local Church must try to discover the specific will of God for them and must show forth in time the mystery of their eternal vocation and learn the 'new name' under which they are to glorify the Blessed Trinity. If the Church is to discover the form that her incarnation in a given people should take, she will have to study, not merely their racial and psychological characteristics, but much more their spiritual and religious preparation which is all to be gathered up in the Paschal mystery. This will apply with all the more force in the case of those peoples who have been particularly favoured by God.

It is therefore unquestionably the duty of the Church in India to read, in the presence and in the name of the Lord, all that has been 'written of her' in the cultural and religious traditions of India, since in the mysterious foreknowledge of the Spirit they have foretold and prepared for her coming. In the Scriptures which are the source of these traditions she will discover the special manner in which she is to glorify the Lord; for, as was said of Abraham in the book of Ecclesiasticus, in words which the liturgy applies to every 'Confessor', "there was none found like him"—each one is unique and irreplaceable in the mystery of the Love of God.

Certainly when these traditions pass over into the sphere of evangelical faith, some things will have to be pruned away and purified, "so that the branch may bring forth more fruit" (John 15:2). This was true of the Mosaic Law even though it had been revealed by God, and it will equally apply to the 'Scriptures of the Gentiles'.

The Biblical text chosen for the following day was to provide us with the key to this transposition and the process of refinement in Christ.

The Gentiles in the Bible

The removal of the veil

This text was the great passage in the second Epistle to the Corinthians (chapters 3 and 4), in which St Paul explains that when the Jews read the Old Testament there is as it were a veil over their hearts. This veil prevents them from perceiving in it the true meaning intended by the Spirit and the mystery of Christ to which it bears witness. The apostle goes on to say, however, that when a man turns to the Lord, the veil is removed. Only Jesus can open a man's mind to understand the Scriptures (Luke 24:45). just as he alone has power to "break the seals of the Book" (Rev. 5:9).

At Nagpur we studied the Scriptures of India in the perspective of a 'theology of fulfilment' which in those days was widely accepted. From that viewpoint all the scriptures of the Cosmic Covenant are seen as finding their true and final meaning in Christ the Lord and in the Pleroma that is inseparable from him. As Paul says in the same passage (2 Cor. 3:17), "the Lord is the Spirit", and it is the Spirit who leads to Christ. All that is luminous in the Scriptures of India must have been placed there in preparation for the 'coming' of the Lord by the Spirit—the Spirit who "searches all things, yea, the deep things of God" (1 Cor. 2:10). The Spirit is the Revealer of the Lord, and there is no time and no place in the universe in which he is not carrying out his mission. This mission has its origins in eternity. The first sign of it is discerned at the very moment of creation, in his hovering over the primordial waters (Gen. 1:2). The Spirit also reveals the Lord in the very mystery of his Person, and little by little unveils his presence to men in the measure in which they are capable of receiving him. But it was only when the Word of God had himself become man and made known to his brethren in human language the secret of his life in the bosom of the Father, that the Spirit could at last reveal in its full splendour the mystery which hitherto he had only been able to disclose in gradual stages. The Spirit could not be given in his fullness until Jesus had been glorified (cp. John 7:39). Scripture also gives us to understand that the gates of heaven—the heaven that is 'above' and the heaven in the depths of oneself—remained closed until Jesus had himself entered the heavenly sanctuary through the 'veil' of his body (Heb. 10:20).

When the destined moment comes for India also, the Upanishadic 'revelation' will at last disclose its final and eschatological meaning. The sign of this will surely be given in the person of one of India's own sons. Such a one will follow the path of the rishis, penetrating into the depths of his own being to the fountain-head of the great experience; and there, in the deepest centre of himself, he will encounter the glory of him who said "Let light shine out of darkness", and the shining of the glory of God in the face of Jesus Christ will transform him into the same glory (2 Cor. 4:6; 3:18). It will be a Christian such as this, a steadfast believer in the Lordship of Christ and at the same time an authentic heir of the sages and spiritual 'patriarchs' of India, who will become the true corner-stone of the Church of India, setting the seal upon the predestination of his ancestors.

Our Christian reading of the Upanishads is strongly reminiscent of the way in which the inspired scribes of Israel constantly 're-read' the earlier Biblical texts with new understanding, of which so many traces can be seen in the Old Testament. For, as the teaching of the prophets gradually made itself felt, and as the sages in their meditations became increasingly open and attentive to the Spirit, so the ancient texts were illuminated for them with new truth and revealed secrets which earlier generations had been incapable of discovering. The climax of this process of re-reading was the Greek translation known as the Septuagint. Then came Jesus; and the Apostles, guided by his teaching and inspired by his Spirit, now received in all fullness (John 7:39; ch.14ff), found a depth of truth in the words of the Old Testament beyond the reach of the earlier prophets. After them the Church, in her liturgical prayer, has continued to read the psalms and the prophetical books with fresh eyes and vision sharpened by the Spirit. As century succeeds century and new people and races are joined to her, she finds in those Scriptures ever new treasures of praise and adoration and an ever deepening realization of the mystery of God. Jerome's Vulgate is an especially authoritative witness to this kind of Christian re-reading of the ancient prophecies.

It is the same for the Christian who takes up the sacred texts of India. But he must not rest content with a hasty and superficial adaptation to his own beliefs of certain isolated words and phrases, after the manner of the 'interpretations' in which the scribes of Qumran took such delight. It is the very thought of the rishis that he must seek to arrive at, making it his own and exploring it to its depths, even to the point of making it explode as it were from within, until its whole import, long prepared by the Spirit, becomes plain. But this can never happen, unless the Christian is willing to enter into and dwell within that 'cave of the heart' where the experience of non-duality wells up and where, even more mysteriously, the Spirit murmurs to his spirit that he too is 'a son' (Rom 8:16).

The Fullness of Christ

The Thursday morning session was centred on the first chapter of the Epistle to the Colossians, taking into account the parallel texts of Ephesians.

These texts reminded us once more that nothing in heaven or on earth can be excluded from the preeminence and the fullness of the Lord Christ "All authority in heaven and on earth has been given to me," said Jesus, when about to leave the world. As John made clear in his Gospel, so Paul in Colossians explains that this preeminence and fullness existed even before the Incarnation; the Lord's sovereignty transcends time. He is himself the Beginning, for in him all things were willed, predestined, given reality and called into being and into the sphere of grace. He is also the End, on whom all things converge, in the cosmos and in history, as well as in the life of each individual. In him all things 'subsist', are held together. He is the ultimate and only explanation, the *raison d'être,* of all that is and all that comes to be. In him all things come forth from the Father, and in him all returns to the Father (cp. 1 Cor.15:28). To crown all, as Paul says in that amazing verse in Colossians (2:9) "in him," in his theandric being, "the whole fullness of the godhead dwells bodily."

His Church proceeds from him and, in its own manner, is his 'fullness' or completion. He has reconciled all things to God, delivering them from the power of darkness, both in heaven and on earth. The Church is precisely this gathering together of all men and all creation, the realization, the restoration upon the earth and in time of that fullness which is the mystery of God in his eternity.

In the universe all things are already bound together and interdependent. All things were contained in the original atom from which the whole cosmos developed, and all will be recovered, perfectly fulfilled and as it were raised to a new level of being, when signs give place to reality in the final consummation. This is equally true of the spiritual order, of which the cosmic order is simply the outward sign and substructure. Here too everything points to a unity both of origin and end; everything comes from and returns to the Fullness. All things are in movement towards the final revelation of the glory of the Lord at the last day, and the universal ingathering of "all in one", of which the Church herself is the prophetic sign and her Eucharistic assembly the sacramental foretaste.

All generations of men, all empires, civilizations, religious traditions, the intuitions of sages and the visions of seers, all have had Christ as their goal. Nothing can withdraw itself from his supremacy, nothing can escape the impulsion of the Spirit which bears everything on earth and in heaven towards the summing up, the 'recapitulation', of all things in Christ who will at last be "all in all" (Col. 3:11), and indeed to the even more mysterious consummation when, in and with Christ, all things are subjected to the Father, so that God may be "all in all" (1 Cor. 15:28).

In our group it was hardly necessary to insist on the importance of these texts as a help in recognizing the presence of the Lord everywhere in the world, his 'pre-existence' in the cosmos and in human societies even before his incarnation, his presence too in those who have not yet been touched by his message.

However, during the discussion which followed the reading of these texts the point which was particularly brought out was that the restoration or recapitulation of all things in Christ is essentially also a work of separation, a work of reconciliation with God through grace, or, as St Paul puts it in the same context, a work of deliverance from the power of darkness. It would not be according to the Christian faith and the teaching of the Bible to expect a smooth and effortless ascent of man and the universe to God. The Cross is at the centre of history, and nothing can come to God save through the Cross of Christ. Sin is a reality which has set its mark on the whole human family and only too often spoilt man's greatest achievements. On the other hand, the revelation of sin—for without revelation how could man really know himself to be a sinner?—has itself disclosed to man the depths of his own being and the real meaning of his existence as a person. As the tempter quite correctly pointed out (Gen. 3:5), man is in a sense equal to God in being able to choose his eternal destiny. This means that each man has an inalienable part to play in the final restoration of all things in Christ, for this can only be achieved through the active cooperation of every individual in the redemption wrought by the Saviour. Man must take a personal part in the redemptive Passover—the 'passing-over' to God—by completely transcending himself and, so to speak, going beyond the utmost limits of his possibilities, both as man and as creature. In the mystery of faith and of repentance he must surrender himself entirely into the hands of God (Ps. 31:5; Luke 23:46) and, by a kind of 'transformation' of his whole being into grace, submit himself wholly to the good pleasure of the Father.

The passage from the Vedantic experience to the experience of the glory of God in Christ Jesus, of which we had spoken on the previous day, is impossible without this leap of faith. There is here a breach of continuity, and grace alone can bring a man to 'the further shore'. But this leap into the future is at one and the same time and indistinguishably God's act and man's act, which must never be thought of as the result of two separate activities supplementing each other and in some sense 'added together'. In the Paschal perspective all is 'theandric', at once wholly of God and wholly of man.

The nearer anyone comes in his spiritual experience to the ultimate revelation of the Glory, the greater will be the danger of his situation, if he refuses to make the leap of faith and rejects the true and living God, on the mistaken plea of preserving the experience which 'he' has gained of God. Anything which has not yet passed over into Christ remains in danger of falling back into darkness, for, as we were reminded on the same day by the Iśa Upanishad, "far deeper is the darkness of him who thinks he knows than of him who is simply ignorant."

The closer one has been brought to the Glory, the more profound will be that darkness—as with the sin of Lucifer, the son of the dawn (Is. 14:12).

In connection with this text and that of the previous day the question was raised whether we Christians, and especially those of us who are ministers of the Gospel, are living withness of the Glory for all to see, giving a flawless reflection of its splendour? Do we genuinely transmit the radiance which comes forth from the Father and is to penetrate everywhere, illuminating the whole universe and all who inhabit it, "increasing unto the perfect day" of the heavenly Jerusalem? Only if that light shines within our own hearts, transforming us from within, can we hope to pierce the darkness and become ourselves a source of light, springing up from the depths of our being, for those of our brothers who still "sit in darkness and the shadow of death" (Luke 1:79). The light must be the light of the Spirit within us, not a merely borrowed light, reflected from without. Too often the chief reason for the failure of our apostolate and the lack of response to our proclamation of the Gospel is simply the absence of this light which we, called to be in Paul's phrase (Eph. 5:8) "sons of the light," should not only reflect but *be* ourselves.

5
THE INTUITIONS OF THE RISHIS

IN our reading of the Upanishads we decided to take the Iśa and the Kena in their entirety, rather than a selection of isolated texts. We chose these two, which come first in the canonical series, because they seemed especially suitable for a first attempt at the contemplative reading of the sacred texts of the Vedānta in a Christian milieu.

In the first place, they have the advantage of being short and relatively easy. The great primitive Upanishads, the Chāndogya and the Brihadāraṇyaka, are no doubt incomparable witnesses to the awakening of the soul to the mystery of being and of the self, and these earliest formulations of that experience have never been surpassed. However, they are very long, and their message is often inextricably entangled in psychological and cosmological speculations which are somewhat disconcerting for the modern reader. The Iśa and Kena Upanishads belong to the period immediately following the great Upanishads. They repeat their authentic message, but in a form that is more condensed and easier to assimilate. The Upanishads of the third period, the Muṇḍaka and the Kaṭha, for instance, are extremely interesting, and it was agreed that they should certainly be meditated upon at length in later meetings. However, even though they faithfully transmit the essential message, they introduce new problems and speculations which later developed into the Sāmkhya and Yoga systems of philosophy. At this stage the mystery of the person, *puruṣa*, obsessed the minds of thinkers and interfered with their meditations on *ātman-brahman*. They were groping after the mystery (not yet clearly perceived as such) of God as 'other', dimly discerned both in and beyond the mystery of the *advaita-ekatvam*, the non-duality and unity of being—a problem for which no thinker, either in India or anywhere else in the world, will ever discover an adequate solution until he has been enlightened by the revelation of the 'face-to-face' of the Father and the Son in the essential *ekatvam*, which is the unity of the Spirit. These Upanishads, then, are also admirably suited for a Christian 're-reading', and it is certain that Christian readers will feel more at home with them, even on a first acquaintance, than with the more ancient texts. However, it seemed better to begin with Upanishads which introduce us to the *atman-brahman* with the all the uncompromising rigour of the advaitic statements. In this way we would avoid the temptation of superficiality, and at the same time lay a solid foundation for a future Christian interpretation of the advaitic experience.

No attempt will be made here to provide a translation of these Upanishads or a continuous commentary on them. Even the quotations from them will be more in the nature of paraphrases. Everyone has the opportunity to read and meditate on them for himself, if not in the original, at least in a translation. The thoughts suggested here, being a summary of what was said at Nagpur, aim above all at helping the reader to attend to their fundamental intuitions and preparing the way for the contact which will surely be established between his spirit and that of the seer whose experience is summed up in the Upanishad.

That which is beyond all

The Kena Upanishad can be regarded as the teaching of a guru who is seeking to awaken his disciple's mind and intelligence to reality—teaching which is interrupted here and there by the reflections, expressed or sometimes surmised, of his pupil.

We should not, however, expect to find here a connected series of propositions logically deduced one from another. The verses of this Upanishad—and this applies even more to the Iśa—are rather a succession of intuitions whose interconnection will not always be clear to those who are only familiar with the ponderous tread of conceptual thought. The logic of the Upanishads is of quite another order. In them everything—words, the order of words, the sequence or non-sequence of ideas—is aimed rather at shattering the accepted categories of perception and judgement in which we normally make ourselves at home. These categories certainly succeed in transmitting some echo of the Real, but just because this echo is itself so satisfying, they very often prevent a man from going further and plunging headlong, so to speak, into the final reality. But the object of the Upanishad is precisely to make us go beyond everything that gives satisfaction. It therefore seeks to get through to the spirit of man by a series of touches, prods and shocks. The effect is like subtle but powerful waves, conveyed by the words, the images, the symbols, even the harshness of style and the disconcerting shifts to different levels of the macrocosm (the universe) and the microcosm (man). These waves come to us across the ages, piercing through time, space and cultural differences. Originating in souls which themselves have entered into the depth, they seek to arouse a similar resonance in the very depth of other souls. Like a diamond drill which nothing can withstand, they pierce deeper and deeper, until at last in those depths the awakening occurs, the archetype is revealed, and contact of the self with the Self takes place beyond every image and every intermediary. This is why purely intellectual disciplines will always be an inadequate preparation for understanding the message of the Upanishads—at least as inadequate as they are for hearing the message which comes to us through Isaiah or St John. It is with the heart alone that a man can 'hear' it, when he shares that condition of receptive awareness in which it was originally received by the rishis of old.

In a word, the Upanishads do not seek to give information, to impart conceptual knowledge or ideas which a man only has to store away in some corner of his memory. Their aim is to help the disciple himself to reach the fundamental experience which defies every attempt at conceptual expression, to put him into the attitude of mind and heart which will make him capable of this experience. This means freeing him from all that his reason continually superimposes on the Real, all those symbols and conceptualizations through which he imagines that he can lay hold of it and 'possess' it. Thus he is gradually brought to that state of total peace and relaxation, pure receptivity and expectancy, emptied of all thought, desire and volition, a simple transparency, which alone will permit the Real to manifest itself in him in all its fullness.

The first question which the guru in the Kena Upanishad asks, or rather invites the disciple to ask himself, is: "What is it that lies behind thought, breath, speech, sight and hearing? What is at their source? What sets them in motion?"

Vedic tradition attributed to the *devas* (the *dii* or *theoi* of the Mediterranean peoples) all the energies at work in the universe and in man. The devas were supposed to rule over the elements and the processes of nature, and equally over the physical and mental activities of man. India had in fact discovered wonderful correspondences and correlations (the original sense of the word *upaniṣad*) between the various levels at which these processes and activities manifest themselves. These correlations all pointed towards the ultimate correlation— the supreme *upaniṣad*—between the innermost principle in man, ātman, and that of the cosmos in its entirety, brahman. "Who then is the deva who gives impetus to sight and hearing? Who harnesses them? Who is the source and origin of their functioning?" Thus the guru invites the disciple to go back to the eye of the eye, the thought of thought, "the see-er of sight, the knower of knowledge," as the Bṛhadāraṇyaka Upanishad had already expressed it; "that which sees in the eye, that which breathes in breath, yet that which the eye cannot see, nor the thought think, nor the breath stir;" "the unseen seer, the unheard hearer, the unthought thinker" (Br. Up. 3.7.16-23).

However far back man tries to go in analysing his biological or psychological functions, or the physiological or mental activities which reveal him to himself and to others, he eventually finds that his way is blocked and he can go no further. For none of these functions, including thought which is the highest of them, is capable of retracing the road back to its source, to the point at which it comes into existence. Like man himself when he tries to grasp himself in his empirical consciousness, they are aware of themselves as functioning, but the impulse which causes them to function eludes them.

Behind the devas of the psychological or cosmosogical order there is another 'deva', a power which is greater than them all. It is only through their participation in this primordial deva, this universal ultimate power, that they themselves are devas at all. This ultimate mystery of being is given by the Vedic tradition the name of brahman. Whatever may be the etymological or primitive meaning of this term, in the Upanishadic period it stood above all for the mystery, the ineffable reality which lies hidden behind all things and yet penetrates all things, that which is at the source of everything that exists, the absolute at once beyond and at the heart of the relative, the limitless both beyond and within every limit, the sacred, the numinous, which is revealed in the ultimate secret of all.

From the fourth verse onwards the Upanishad develops into a regular litany of triumph, celebrating the progressive discovery of brahman in the depths of and beyond each of the devas, hearing, breathing, seeing "It is this which is Brahman," repeats the guru like a refrain, "and not what a vain and ignorant people imagines and adores as such."

There comes a point in the interior life when we have to pass beyond everything, even the world of concepts which, while it helps us to know God, "the Real of the Real" (Br.Up., 2.1.20), no less surely conceals him from us. God is none of the things that man thinks about him, nothing that man experiences of him. Only in this 'nothing', in pure naked faith, is he truly found. This was the teaching of John of the Cross which he learnt through his own profound experience.

"He is risen, he is not here." He is not in the tomb in which men thought to confine him, to keep him safe that they might worship him in comfort. The shroud and grave-clothes, in which the soul in its love had wrapped his body, are still there. But he has made his escape, and nothing can hold him back. The heavy stone which no human power could remove without the help of grace, has been rolled away—the angel of the resurrection made it leap from its place, as though by a mere touch of his finger.

And now the Lord himself has 'risen' at last in the deepest centre of my being, beyond the reach of any idea I could ever have formed of him, at a depth whose very existence within me I could never have suspected.

"Woman, whom seekest thou?...the living among the dead?" As if the living God could ever be held in a rigid framework of concepts! And you who share in his very life, why do you tarry on these merely superficial levels of your being, where you are seeking to 'touch' and 'feel' him? Truly, he is risen, and has appeared to Simon—Simon, son of Jonas, whose faith upholds the Church—and to you also, in your own depths, in purest faith.

"I laid me down and slept, and rose up again" (Ps. 3:5). I fell asleep, and was as though sunk in deepest slumber. Now I have wakened, I have discovered God and, in the very mystery of God, I find the truth of being, my own truth.

But this Brahman cannot be reached by any deva. He is other than what is known, and yet still further above and beyond what is not known. The second chapter of the Upanishad plays wonderfully upon these paradoxes:

> If you think, "I know him,"
> in truth you know very little of this Brahman,
> of what you are of him,
> of what there is of him in the devas.
> He is not known by him who knows him,
> not understood by him who understands him;
> he alone contemplates him, who has ceased to contemplate him.
> It is in all knowledge, as though by intuition,

that the wise man finds him.
It is in him alone, the ātman, that each one is strong;
it is by knowing him alone that one becomes immortal...
Great, in truth, is the loss
of that man who does not attain him here below.

Such then is the ultimate mystery of man. Such is the true nature of the divine and sacred reality to which we should turn, and which even more we should seek to know in lofty contemplation, leaving aside those mere projections of our own thought, with which men too often rest content, though they never lead to Reality itself.

Chapter 3 takes up the same idea, now in the form of a striking fable.

The devas were proud of themselves, their powers and their achievements. By means of the external senses, they had placed the whole universe within man's grasp. Intelligence and physical strength were progressively bringing under his control the entire cosmos, from the infinite smallness of the atom to the infinite vastness of space. By the power of thought man had given meaning to all that he perceives in the world, and in imagination he had even created other worlds. Finally, through self-consciousness he had become aware of himself in all the mystery of his personality and his freedom.

The devas ruled supreme in both the cosmic and the psychological orders. Quite naturally they took the credit for all that happens there.

To put them to confusion and make them realize their 'vanity' Brahman one day showed himself to them. But the devas did not recognize him. They asked each other who this 'spirit' could be.

Agni was deputed to find out—Agni, Fire, which certain commentators interpret as physical force and bodily energy.

Brahman asked Agni: "Who are you? What can you do?" "I am Agni," he replied; "Jātavedas, he who knows the origin of all things. Nothing on earth can escape my power. I burn up everything."

"Very well, burn this," said Brahman simply, and threw down in front of him a wisp of straw.

Agni flung himself upon the straw with all his might, but was unable to burn it. He went back to the devas and acknowledged his failure.

Next they sent Vāyu, the Wind, the vital force in man. He also boasted before Brahman about his strength.

"Then blow this away" said Brahman, placing before him the

same wisp of straw. Vāyu blew as hard as he could, but the straw never moved.

Then Indra, the king of the devas, went to meet this mysterious being—Indra who is the power of the human mind, man's thought, his consciousness, the highest point that the universe has attained to in man. But when Indra drew near to Brahman, Brahman vanished.

Nothing in the cosmos or in man has power, energy or effectiveness apart from *That*, the one who is the source of all power, and who is at work in every activity, whether cosmic or human. When man, by the use of his mind, tries even to recognize this power which is behind, beyond and within everything, the 'phantom', or idea which the deva had conceived of this 'spirit', has already disappeared. He eludes every thought of man,

> other than thinking, beyond non-thinking,
> unknown when he is known,
> only recognized when everything has disappeared....

At that moment, the fable continues, in the ethereal space in which Brahman had vanished, there appeared a brilliant form—Umā, the daughter of the Snows. Indra asked her, " Who was that 'spirit' who has just disappeared?"

Umā revealed to him that it was Brahman. "Through him alone" she said, "you devas won the victory, the power to rule in the world and in man. Truly it is him alone that you have any right to be proud." Umā is the highest wisdom, the fine point of the human spirit, the furthest reach of the intellect, which is somehow in contact with both the lower and the upper world, with the soul in its unsearchable depths and also with its outward and visible effects. Umā is not unlike what Śrī Aurobindo in his vision of the world calls "the supra-mental"; she is that 'spark' of which the mediaeval western mystics spoke, and even perhaps a sign of the Spirit *(pneuma)* which according to the New Testament reveals to our spirits. as if from within, the secret of their origin in the bosom of the Father (Rom. 8:16).

Even the name of Brahman, the Absolute, has to be revealed to man's mind; of himself he is quite incapable of discovering it. There has to be some intermediary between this ineffable being and the human consciousness, between man in the depths of his being and his self-manifestation in his faculties of knowledge and action. Of this inmost mystery nothing can be put into words, says the Kaṭha Upanishad, except *"asti"*, "it *is*" (6.12); *"tad etad iti"*—*"That is it!"*

is all that can truly be said of this ineffable supreme felicity..." (5.14), that is, the joy and peace in the soul which follow upon even a secret contact with Brahman (cp., Kena Up., 4.3). Solely by its effects the presence of Brahman is known.

When a Christian reads this Upanishad and reflects upon the mysterious and brilliant form which appears in the centre of the heaven of the soul, shining with the radiance of the immense virgin snows and revealing to man the name of *Brahman* which is all that can be said of him, the Absolute, then he is bound to recall that light which gradually filtered into the minds of the inspired scribes of Israel and prepared them for the final revelation. That light enabled them more and more clearly to discern the mystery of Yahweh's presence (the *shekinah*), his glory (*qabod*), his holiness and apartness (*qadosh*), and eventually, his wisdom. And this wisdom, radiant and almost personified (Wis. 6:12), is like a sign of the double 'procession' within the heart of God: of the Son, the Word "proceeding from the mouth of the Most High" (Ecclus 24:3), who would reveal through human lips and in human language the very name and secret of God—and of the Spirit, who opens man's ear from within to hear his Word and makes him understand this Name, henceforth inscribed upon his very heart (Rev. 3:12).

A fourth chapter brings this Upanishad to an end.

What is the sign of this Brahman at the level of the devas and of human perception?

"Is is (the cry), Ah! (that one utters) when the lightning flashes, Ah! when the eyes have blinked" (4.4).

The lightning flashes—Ah! The eyes blink—Ah! That is all. Brahman has passed. We did not see his face, for that is impossible, but we felt his presence. In some mysterious way a man is never the same again, when he has once felt the touch of Brahman.

There follows a further attempt to explain the nature of the self at the level of the *atman*. The sentence is obscure, but in the light of 2.4, it may be paraphrased as follows: "The discovery of brahman (or the awareness of the self) is that towards which the mind is ceaselessly moving; and then, all of a sudden, 'That' takes form in a thought" (4.5).

God is surely that reality, present to the inmost depths of our spirit, though always beyond our reach, who nevertheless calls and draws us to himself irresistibly. All the words we apply to him, all the thoughts we think of him and all the forms in which we contemplate him, are hopelessly unsatisfying and in the end leave us with a sense of frustration. We even succeed at times in reducing what he has revealed of himself to commonplaces, emptied of the mystery. Therefore, when 'the lightning flashes', our mind is conscious only of a great emptiness. Our spirit no longer seeks to encounter God as a Presence; all forms have vanished, and it succeeds in grasping nothing but itself. The Lord then makes himself known far more as an Absence than as a Presence... He is in everything, yet he is beyond everything. Instinctively, unwearyingly, the mind tries everywhere to discover him; but, as the Upanishad says, when thought arrives at the point where it hoped to find him, he has already departed. Yet still there remains in the mind the memory of that 'lightning-flash'. However certainly it knows 'That' to be beyond its reach, it never for a moment ceases to strain towards it. It cannot help itself; it is obsessed by this absence which is a Presence, this darkness which both hides and reveals the light—that light which springs up of itself in him who has consented to be only darkness.

The Upanishad continues: "The secret name of 'That', of the Brahman which cannot be defined, is *'tadvanaṃ'*—'that desire,' 'that delight,' or rather, 'the desire of That', 'the delightfulness of That,'—

>in the depth of all things, as that which arouses all desire,
>in the depth of all things, as that which bestows and fulfils all joy.

"Master, now tell me the upanishad!" pleads the disciple at this point. He is no doubt hoping to receive some additional instruction, some more ideas through which he trusts incorrigibly that he will attain to the knowledge of Brahman.

"You have heard the upanishad already," replies the guru in a tone of finality. "Indeed we have told you the upanishad of Brahman."

In reality, what more could be said? He who has known the 'lightning-flash' in the depths of his being—he alone has genuinely 'heard' the upanishad of Brahman. There really is no sign of Brahman other than this lightning-flash!

With the method of the guru of the Kena Upanishad one cannot help comparing that of Ramana Maharshi. When a disciple came to ask him for instruction, the sage invariably replied with the single question: "*Who are you? Who* is asking such and such a question?"

The disciple was not expected to answer by giving his name or that of his family—purely external things which in any case we only learn from others. What the Maharshi intended was that he should compel his thinking to turn inward upon itself in order to discover the thinker. In this there was no question of making a logical analysis of the idea of the self, but rather of the spirit journeying inward and seeking as it were to get behind its immediate level of consciousness—a process to be repeated as long as necessary. The Maharshi promised that the moment could not fail to come when this consciousness 'in search of itself' would vanish as though by magic for ever, and the essential and unique 'I' would shine henceforth with its own brilliance in the firmament of the soul. Śri Ramaṇa did not even envisage the arrival of an Umā to enlighten Indra, for at the moment of awakening to the *I*, Indra himself—understanding, thought, consciousness—will vanish.

The Upanishads, as we have just said, are not 'works of reference' or 'portmanteaus of ideas'; still less is the Indian guru a man who has passed an examination and obtained his teacher's diploma. He is one who *knows* by personal experience, one who is capable of establishing contact with the inmost soul of his disciple and of communicating to him mysteriously, by his 'grace', that same experience. The disciple must be so pure and transparent, so open and teachable, that the words uttered by the guru can penetrate to his inmost heart and there spring up like a perpetual fountain of living water.

The aim is not to discover the superficial 'me' which, like every other mental or material object, is inexorably carried away in the flux of cosmic evolution. What one has to exert oneself to recognize and bring to the surface of consciousness is the real 'me', the very mystery of the person. No doubt this real 'me' is in fact inseparable from the bodily and mental circumstances accompanying its manifestation in the world; but it infinitely transcends them and enjoys such liberty in their regard that even death itself cannot affect it. This is surely the mystery of that 'new name' by which God calls each of us, as a unique person, to being and to glory—to his own Being and Glory.

Having given this call to man, God does not allow him to stop halfway on the road to the discovery of himself—herein we see the reason for the existence of time. He does not permit the creature whom he has invited to be eternally his 'son', to remain indefinitely on the surface of himself, for ever identifying himself with his physical or social activities in the evolution of the world and of history. So too he does not allow him to stop short at the forms and signs through which he conducts his relations with God, his 'religion'. In mysterious ways the Lord intervenes, causing man to experience a kind of inner frustration, even in the midst of his greatest successes in the physical, intellectual or spiritual spheres. For none of these things is God—they are merely signs of his presence. Nor are they man, as he truly is. Blown up with pride in their great achievements, the devas forget that there is a mystery even greater than themselves.

Then God in his mercy sends his messengers—night, darkness, suffering, disablement, failure in the eyes of the world. He gives a 'sign' to man, and waits. The devas are disturbed by this sign which they do not understand, appearing like a spectre within the narrow horizons of their vision. Who is this newcomer? What does he think he is doing? Why must he interfere? We were getting on so well without him!

Popular religion finds it quite natural to be satisfied with rites and formulas. "Let there be an agreement between us and God! We will offer him all the sacrifices that he has prescribed. But then let him leave us in peace. He may also give us a nice simple catechism and a well formulated theology, free from obscure ideas. We will gladly recite the Creeds and confess, for example, that there is only One God in three Persons, and that the Word was made flesh, died and rose again. But we hope he will limit his requirements to this and will not expect these formulas to make any impression on our thinking or our lives!" Popular religion comforts and satisfies men; but only too often it empties out the essential restlessness implanted by God in the heart. On the other hand, the secret and irresistible attraction of the unknown poses questions which remain for ever unanswered. He who thinks he understands, understands nothing but his own thought. There is no possible response except to 'take off'. Without dying there is no passage beyond death.

From the depths of the soul, from the silence at the source of being, rises the fundamental question: "Who am I?" This very question is itself the revelation of Brahman.

For this question reduces the spirit to silence, a silence which is itself Reality and Truth. This is the Silence from which the Word sprang forth in the bosom of the Father, as Ignatius of Antioch reminded the Magnesians. But this Word is uttered and heard at a level of the self which transcends the phenomenal consciousness. It is not a word born of human thought or the human mind, but the very Word in which

The Intuitions of the Rishis

all things have their source, the Vedic OM, the primordial utterance. It is the Logos, the Word through whom all things were made, in whom, at the 'dawn' of eternity (if one may so express it), the Father, the Source and Beginning, awoke to himself.

To attain to the Self is to attain supreme Bliss; for Bliss, *ananda*, as the Taittirīya Upanishad says, is the deepest level of being, the innermost 'sheath' of the atman, the Self. The Upanishads constantly identify Bliss with immortality, the ultimate object of desire for all conscious beings. "Know and revere *That* as *tadvanam*, that delight", concludes the Kena. Towards *That* all creatures are drawn, for *That* they yearn. He who has attained to this Bliss in himself has truly become the centre of the universe, a centre within the unique Centre. Out of his own fullness he radiates the fullness of Bliss, *ananda*, *tadvanam*, having become a living source of love and joy, at which all who wish can come and slake their thirst.

He alone is a true guru who has discovered this source within himself and therefore is able in his turn to be a source for others.

It is hardly necessary to make more explicit the Christian mystery which can be traced like a golden thread through this Upanishad.

There seems to be yet another parallel which could be drawn. The manner in which the Kena causes thought to rise above its natural level to a mysterious Beyond is somewhat reminiscent of the general lines of what are known in the West as the proofs for the existence of God.

However, in the East, when thought discovers that which is transcendent, it refuses to reason about or name this Beyond. All it will say is "That is it, *tad.*" Certainly it is supreme Bliss; it is a lightning-flash; but nothing more can be said. To name It would be to lose it. Nor would anyone venture to say that here is 'thought' and there, over against it, is *That*; for who indeed is left that might think '*That*'? What place is left in the thought for a 'thinker' other than *That* itself? This however does not amount to affirming that they are identical, for that again would be to form an idea, and in that same instant Brahman would have vanished.

In the Chāndogya Upanishad this was called *advaita*, non-duality, the absolute negation of any kind of differentiation whatever, the recognition that thought is incapable of reaching beyond intself. On the other hand, the Iśa speaks of *ekatvam*, unity, By this expression it indicates the universal and unique presence of *That*, the Real in itself, which is ultimately the only thing that the wise man beholds in everything that he perceives. Here once more we meet the great contrast between the spiritual attitude of the Western sage and that of his Eastern brother. Both alike have discovered in the depth of their souls a mystery which is beyond their grasp. The former cannot rest until he has given this mystery a name, or at least, like Jacob at the fords of Jabbok (Gen. 32:28), until he has striven to wrest its name from it. Never can he forget that it *confronts* him, whether he stands before it in the pride of his manhood, or kneels in adoring recognition of his own creatureliness, or is humbled in the awareness that he is a forgiven sinner. But when the Eastern sage comes in contact with that mystery, he remains silent. He cannot even adore, because for this he would at least need to be able to think of himself as somehow apart from it—but in the secret and infinite space of his heart, what possibility is there for any thought to arise?

It was in the West that, in the Biblical perspective, the 'Word of God' was revealed to mankind. We may then say that it was with a view to preparing the world for hearing the Word of God that the religious thought of the West was allowed to take the direction that it did. However it seems that the time has come to reintegrate into the Christian consciousness the complementary approach of the East, so that when these two modes of experience come together in Christian hearts, they may mutually refine each other and be set free from the limitations which each inevitably entails. The perfect prototype of the complete experience is the mystery of the Blessed Trinity itself, at once a supreme unity in the Spirit, and also the very source of this unity, the mysterious 'face-to-face' of the Father and the Son. We might well say that the Church will only be able to reveal this mystery in its fullness when she has at last integrated into her own experience, in the person of her Indian sons, that dimension of non-duality beyond all words which the Spirit has preserved in them with her in view.

That which is all in all

The Iśa Upanishad is especially well known. It stands at the head of the canonical Upanishads. It is very brief—a single chapter—and is in verse. Some of its *ślokas* border on paradox, and it does not easily lend itself to an immediate synthesis. While faithfully echoing the purely Vedantic teaching of the earlier Upanishads, it also shows some recognition of the path of 'works', thus preparing the way for the teaching of the Bhagavad-Gītā. What is even more significant, it uses the masculine pronoun in speaking of the Absolute, the That *(tad)* of

The Intuitions of the Rishis

the Kena; it also shows scant respect for the *vidya*, the 'knowledge', to which so many so-called sages allow themselves to become attached.

The more difficult verses of this Upanishad will not be lingered over now, any more than they were at Nagpur. As with the Kena, we shall simply try to take note of the essential points and the central message. Our purpose will be, as always, to penetrate as deeply as possible into the thought of the rishi and to share, as far as we may, in his actual experience.

The Kena sang of That which is beyond all—so far beyond, that the mind can no longer keep it in view, so as to gaze at it and prostrate before it in adoration. Man loses his balance and as it were suffers shipwreck when he tries to reach out in thought to the Beyond.

The Īśa celebrates That which is All in all—so profoundly interior, that no place is left for man in his inmost being where he may find himself. When he tries to recollect himself and seek his 'centre', he founders no less inevitably.

The Upanishad opens with *"pūrṇam adaḥ, pūrṇam idam"*:

> Fullness everywhere,
> Fullness there, fullness here;
> From fullness comes forth fullness,
> and everywhere, one with itself, there remains fullness.

In the thought of the rishi this certainly means that the whole mystery of Brahman, the Absolute, is revealed to the astonished soul just as fully in its 'manifestation' at the level of sense-perception and thought, as it is in its indescribable hiddenness at the heart of the primordial 'Unmanifested'—an idea which is developed throughout this Upanishad.

The Kena seeks to lead us to the intuition of the Beyond, to realize the inaccessibility of this Presence, whose attainment is however essential to make man fully present to himself. The whole of the Īśa is a meditation upon the mystery of this Presence, this Fullness, as inexplicably both *here* and *there*, the presence and the fullness of absolute Being which transcends all things in its very immanence and is immanent in all things precisely because of its transcendence.

The conviction that the unique and infinite Fullness is also present in our midst saves the author of the Īśa from yielding to a common temptation of Vedāntin intellectuals. In their mistaken anxiety to safeguard the transcendence of the Presence, they too often banish it altogether from the world, which they regard as pure illusion or *māyā*, and therefore as something from which one must free oneself at all costs, if one wishes to attain to the Real.

The Christian who has pondered the Scriptures with an understanding born of the heart will find that this hymn to the Fullness evokes wonderful echoes within his own soul. *Pūrṇam*, Fullness, at once recalls the mystery of the *Pleroma* (Fullness), to which Paul introduced the Church :

> The Father is Fullness, the Son is Fullness,
> Fullness also is the Holy Spirit of God!
> Fullness in heaven, fullness on earth,
> From the infinite glory of this Fullness.
> From him who is Fullness
> He who is Fullness proceeds,
> and proceeds also the Consummation of Fullness,—
> from eternity to eternity one unique Fullness!
> Fullness is God in his eternity,
> Fullness is his Christ,
> who reveals him in time,
> and in whose body dwells
> all the Fullness of the Godhead!
> Fullness is the Lord,
> Fullness is his Church,
> his very body and the Fullness of him
> who, being All in all,
> is himself Fullness!

The first verse of the *Īśa* Upanishad affirms the universal presence of the Lord, *Īsh*, Master, the Power or Might, here personified, whom the Kena showed us as at work in all the activities of the devas:

> In everything that moves,
> Whatever it is in the world that is moving,
> Īsh is dwelling.

The Kena took as the starting-point of its meditation the data of human psychology, and thence soared up to the contemplation of Brahman. The *Īśa* begins from movement, the impermanence of the cosmos, the multiplicity inherent in the universe, and discovers in its very depth the Unmoving, the Permanent, the One.

The Intuitions of the Rishis

> One, unmoving, he is more rapid than the mind.
> The devas try to catch up with him,
> but he is always ahead of them.
> They run after him,
> but without moving he outruns them all.
> He moves, he does not move;
> He is over there, he is here, quite close.
> He is within all that is,
> from all that is he is distinct.
> He is everywhere,
> shining, bodiless, without limbs,
> percipient, wise, born of himself.
> He it is who orders all things aright
> throughout the eternal years.

The Iśa usually gives to That, *tad*, the name of ātman, whereas the Kena normally prefers to call it Brahman.

The ātman is the *self*—grammatically it is the reflexive personal pronoun; it is the principle which constitutes the reality of the person, his awareness of himself. This principle naturally defies any attempt at exhaustive analysis. As indeed the Taittirīya Upanishad explains, the analysis of the self reveals a series of progressively deeper and more subtle principles. Beginning with the material body, "made of food," and passing through those made of breath, thought, intelligence and bliss (which seems to be innermost one), we reach that ultimate and inexpressible secret which explains everything but is explained by nothing, the pure and non-reflex awareness of the self which, however, is never attained until the self is made totally void.

However, as the rishi of the Chāndogya had wonderingly discovered (3.14.3; 3.13.7), this ātman

> within my heart, which is smaller than a grain of rice,
> or a grain of millet, or the kernel of a grain of millet,

is also

> that selfsame light which shines throughout all things,
> throughout the universe,
> throughout the worlds beyond which there is nothing further—
> and it is also the light which shines within the heart of man.

The sage who has experienced within himself the mystery of the Fullness, henceforth sees everywhere nothing but this same fullness:

> *sarvāṇi bhūtāni ātmani.....*

> sarvabhūteṣu ca ātmānam
> he sees all that is in the ātman, the Self,
> and the ātman in all that is.

For him it is as though

> sarvāṇi bhūtāni ātma eva abhūt;
> everything has now become just the Self.

Henceforth in all things he will contemplate the unity, *ekatvam*,—or the non-duality, *advaita*, as it is called in other texts,—which is equally the *pūrṇam*, fullness, of which the opening verse of the Upanishad sang.

Unity, non-duality, fullness— to attempt to explain the mystery in our inevitably limited and limiting concepts would be to desecrate it. Anyone who imagines that he has said everything has certainly missed the essential point... That is why it is so difficult to base a philosophy on the experience of being. And if one does so, then such a philosophy must be regarded, as is traditionally the case in India, as no more than a launching pad for the human spirit, so that it may be able to escape from the pull of earth and take untrammelled flight into infinite space.

As for the man who has had this experience and realized that all things are embraced by the essential unity, no sorrow or illusion can ever again touch him (verse 7). For the supreme Lord, Īsh, is everywhere at home, in the whole world and in every creature, "reaching everywhere, luminous, without body, without limbs, untouched by any evil, wise and all-seeing, as though born of himself, disposing all things rightly throughout the eternal years." (This is verse 8, of which part was quoted above.) In the development of the rishi's thought, this text can be understood just as well of the Spirit who dwells in all men and all things, as of the man who dwells in the Spirit.... St Paul indeed should have accustomed us to certain mysterious equations of this sort, by the ambiguity with which he uses the word *pneuma* (Spirit or spirit).

In these verses, taken as a whole, there is a great lesson which is too often forgotten by the popularizers of Advaita and Vedānta.

In India as in Europe, Advaita and Vedānta have practically come to be taken as a kind of religion or super-religion, in whose name superficial judgements are loftily passed on everything. Then with the so-called Vedantic view of the world as an excuse, the most elementary duties towards others are promptly forgotten or disregarded—a hypocrisy identical with that which Jesus denounced so vigorously in the Pharisees.

In flat contradiction to this, however, verse 6 of the Upanishad says: "He who sees the one ātman in all things does not shrink from anything whatever, feels no aversion towards anything, does not run away from anything."

Jñāna or wisdom is not an escape from the world of action, and the jñānī is not necessarily one who withdraws from society to the solitude of forests or mountains.

The jñānī is a man who has realized the mystery of the self through a deep intuition of which he may even be unaware at the level of conceptual thought. In this intuition he has taken the great leap by which a man reaches the 'further shore' of the self. He has become free from that superficial consciousness of his own individuality which made him regard himself—despite being merely a particular moment in the material and psychic evolution of the universe—as the very centre of the world, and resulted in his treating everyone and everything else as serving the ends of that petty 'self'. Now that he has discovered the true centre of himself in that very principle from which the world itself originates, his 'personal' interests henceforth coincide wholly with the divine plan, according to the Lord's will for the world and everything in it. His own well-being is identical with the well-being of everything else. Thus in a sense he is present everywhere, set free from all that formerly limited him physically and mentally to his surface consciousness. Through the identification of his will with that of the supreme Spirit, he is master of all things; his purpose and his bliss are one with the purpose and bliss of Him who rules the universe.

His life will doubtless continue to follow its normal course—according to his *karma*, as people say in India; or, in Christian terms, according to his personal vocation and the providential circumstances of his earthly pilgrimage. If it happens to be his calling, he may spend his life in solitude and silence, detached from everything, in total freedom. He will then be a sign to other men of the transcendence of the ātman, of its hiddenness and its essential otherness from every conceivable manifestation of itself. But equally the jñānī may remain among men; in which case he will be in their midst as a sign of the universal presence of this same ātman in every moment of its manifestation in time and in every action of its self-revelation through things or through men.

The jñānī will do whatever his companions and colleagues do—only he will do it perfectly. Freed from the limitations of human selfishness and anxiety, in all that he does he will be in a pre-eminent way the instrument of the spirit. He will have a marvellous detachment from everything, because, if the Absolute is present in everything that happens, equally it is not limited to any one thing. If his vocation leads him to the service of his brothers, for example the poor, the lepers, or the underprivileged, he will give himself completely to each of them, totally forgetful of himself; for in each of these needy and unfortunate people he discerns the whole mystery of the Presence. Whether or not he explicitly realizes it, his service will include at the same time the gift of himself to the other as other, in his personal reality and as a unique manifestation of the mystery of the self, and also his gift to the other as one with himself, in a unity that transcends the act of giving. Something of this is surely implied in the parable of the body and its members which all work for each other, as we find it in St Paul (1 Cor. 12) and in the Upanishads (e.g. Kauṣītaki 3). What he does for this brother is done for him quite simply, with no further motive, without seeking any advantage for himself, nor even another advantage of a different order for this man. The only motive for his act of service is the brother himself, in his situation at this moment, constituting as he does a real and determinate expression of the Presence.

This Upanishad should therefore be reflected upon with particular attention by those who believe themselves to be called to follow the way of jñāna. We can be certain that in the case of a true jñānī, charity will be perfect and the gift of self complete. This unfortunately does not apply to those who have no more than an intellectual knowledge of advaita, but who nevertheless claim to be making progress on this path. Their self-centredness is sometimes appalling. They consistently refuse to give themselves to their neighbour, they accept no responsibility for their brothers and are unwilling to serve them in any way. They excuse themselves on the grounds that they have to guard 'their' meditation and their so-called absorption in the ātman. Actually, by thus placing the ātman on one side and the world on the other, they are in practice setting the ātman in opposition with the world; they treat it as belonging to a *dvandva*, or 'pair of opposites', pairing it off with or opposing it to the world. By so doing they strip the ātman of its fullness and of its non-duality. The true ātman, which they claim to have found in their meditations, has in fact eluded them. They are left with nothing but their wretched little self-contred ego, which they imagine to be the supreme Self!

It goes without saying that times of retreat—of 'withdrawal', to borrow the Iśa's term—of solitude and silence, and even of being set free from all forms of 'service', have their rightful place on the path of spiritual progress. Used on appropriate occasions, they are indispensable means for freeing the soul from the hold of external things. But what needs to be stressed here in connection with this Upanishad is that jñāna or advaita in themselves have nothing to do with a particular form of life, for instance, a life of seclusion and continuous meditation. What is more, so long as the would-be spiritual man has not recognized the presence of the One-without-a-second in everything that exists and everything that happens, he has not yet begun to understand the mystery of the ātman. His concentrated thought is dangerously focussed on an empty concept, and in the end it is to himself alone that he is subordinating and sacrificing everything, including the world and his fellow-men.

An anecdote concerning Ramana Maharshi will provide a fitting conclusion to these reflections. A disciple of Mahātma Gandhi went to see him and confided to him his hopes and plans for improving the lot of India's poor. Śrī Ramana interrupted him, saying: "Only one thing is necessary: find out *who* wants to devote himself to this social work. You—who are you? This alone matters." A few minutes later, Śrī Ramaṇa inquired whether the peacocks in the ashram had received their daily ration of grain. Thereupon Ramchandraji (the Gandhian) asked him: "Bhagavān, if you show such concern for the peacocks in your ashram, why do you disapprove if I concern myself with men, my brothers?" As a matter of fact, the Maharshi never on principle recommended a life of solitude or sannyāsa. Without knowing it, he made his own the advice of St Paul: "Let each one remain in the condition in which the Lord has placed him" (cp.1 Cor. 7:17). For him this depended on each man's karma or vocation. The 'realization' of the self has nothing to do with the different occupations in which people are engaged. The essential thing is that, in the midst of one's mental or material occupations, one should keep oneself unattached, 'realizing' oneself as sovereignly free. This was undoubtedly what the sage was trying by the use of paradox to convey to his visitor. He himself was always the first and the most diligent in performing the daily tasks of the ashram, nor did he ever allow his followers to do anything by halves. Least of all did he seek to escape from the crowd in order to safeguard his solitude.

The Christian will study these verses of the Īśa as attentively as does the Hindu, but with added penetration.

In the first place, he will find here a foreshadowing of what the new Testament reveals concerning the universal presence of the Spirit, and a kind of anticipation of the summing up of all things in Christ. The Biblical message will prevent him from interpreting his experience of non-duality as a philosophical *ekatvam*, an ontological 'identification' of God and the creature, as was strongly brought out in the course of our discussion.* It is absolutely essential for him to safeguard, both in his thought and in his formulations of it, the complete liberty of God in his decision to create and the distinction between created being and the uncreated being of God. However, he must equally strongly affirm the *ekatvam*, the oneness in the Spirit of all things, whether in heaven or on earth, the oneness of the mystery of God and the mystery of man. He will be never be entitled to minimize, for example, the "All in all" of God (1 Cor. 15:28), or Christ (or the Spirit?—Eph. 1:23), however incapable our human concepts may be of expressing it. So too he must give full value to the strong expressions used by St Paul when he declares that the risen Christ lives in the Christian (Gal. 2:20), and that henceforth there can be neither Jew nor Greek, neither slave nor free man, but once again only the Lord Christ who is all, and in all (Col. 3:11)

Even less than the sage in the Upanishad will the Christian 'refuse' himself to anything. He will not withdraw from the world into which he has been called, nor from the service of his brothers, in order to serve a 'god of his own devising'; for, as St John teaches in his Epistle, God is to be met first of all in his brother-men. So too, when the Christian monk withdraws into silence and solitude to be more deeply attentive to the presence, he is not running away from or shirking his duty. Christ did not ask his Father to take his disciples out of the world, but to 'protect' them in the world, to 'free' them from the world. The

---

*Even Vedānta will not identify God and the creatures, for the very notion of Creator (included in any concept of God) excludes their identification as contradictory. The Upanishadic equivalence is not between God and man, but between *ātman*, the Self, as revealed in the ultimate experience of self-awareness, and *brahman*, the mystery of the Absolute in itself.

life of a hermit is also a *diakonia*, a service, in the Church. The hermit bears witness in the Church and in the world to the eschatological dimension of the Kingdom—a witness all the more necessary in that the world, and often even the Church, allows itself only too easily to be carried away by the tide of 'becoming'. It is in the name of his brethren and for their sake that the hermit withdraws from their 'presence' in order to be 'in their midst' a standing witness to the truth that God is beyond every sign.

Finally, these verses of the Īśa Upanishad could form the basis for a Christian understanding of Vedānta. They assert with unusual vigour—even if they do not wholly succeed in explaining it—the reality of God's self-manifestation in the world. The world is not devoid of truth or reality; it is not *maya* or illusion, except when it is thought of as separated from the One who reveals himself in it, since its whole reason for existing, its very nature as a sign, consists precisely in making him manifest. Therefore when one wants to distinguish the world from God, one should not say that it lacks reality, but rather, following the great doctors of Vedānta, that it cannot be perceived, defined or grasped by concepts, that it is neither *sat* nor *asat*, neither real nor unreal. The Christian also affirms that the world only exists in God, in the Word, by whom it was made. If it exists, it is by no means after the fashion of something that one fine day was casually launched into being; nor is it a thing which, while it owes its existence to God, is nevertheless far away from him. According to Christian revelation, the world exists in the very depths of God, the most secret and profound abyss of the Father's Love, of which it is the mysterious expression and manifestation.

At this point it will be illuminating to use as a commentary on the Īśa Upanishad a few verses of the Muṇḍaka, which had been read by the group in Delhi at Easter 1963.

According to the Kena, Brahman is at the source of all human perception, while ever remaining inaccessible to perception.

The ātman, adds the Īśa, is motionless in all that moves, one in what is multiple, simultaneously interior and exterior to all things, everywhere identical with itself.

In the Kaṭha and the Muṇḍaka the interiority of this mystery is often symbolized by the image of the cave, *guhā*, the secret place of the heart. For example, the Muṇḍaka (2.2) says that there

> he abides, manifest, quite near,

the dweller in the cave, the great Goal,
the centre of all;
on him are settled all the worlds,
all the inhabitants of the worlds,
everything that moves and winks and breathes.
He, the shining one, is the object of all desire,
tinier than the atom,
beyond the reach of all knowing...

That One is Brahman, the Supreme, the Unchanging,
He is life; he is speech; he is spirit;
He is the Real; he is Immortality.
It is he who is the mark to aim at.
My dear, aim straight for that mark.

Take into your hands the shining bow of the Upanishads;
on it set your arrow
sharpened by meditation.
With your mind stretched towards the unity, bend that bow.
My dear, aim at this mark. It is he, the Unchanging.

OM, the *praṇava*, is the bow;
the arrow is the self,
it is you yourself.
The mark is Brahman.
Aim at it without allowing any distraction.
Fix yourself there, like the arrow in the mark.

He on whom all this world is woven,
heavens and earth, breath and spirit,—
know that that in truth is the unique Self; it is thyself!
Let go all other words;
this is the bridge that leads to non-death.
Greetings to you who pass to the other shore,
beyond the darkness.

Truly Brahman is all this,
Brahman before! Brahman behind!
Brahman on the right, Brahman on the left!
Brahman above, Brahman below!
Only Brahman indeed
in everything and everywhere!

The Īśa Upanishad, in common with many of the others, makes great use of the symbolism of light and darkness to signify respectively the condition of those who have realized the interior mystery and of those who have chosen to remain in the world perceived by the mind and senses, from which there is no escape (*saṁsāra*, the endless cycle of rebirth).

> Worlds there are without sun (or, of the *asuras* or demons);
> To them, on leaving this world,
> depart those who have killed the self (Īśa, verse 3).

He who turns his back on the brilliant light of the atman in the depths of his being resembles one who on the physical level destroys his own life. After that, what can he expect but the darkness of hell?

'Leaving this world' no doubt refers to that 'passing over' which is physical death. But it surely includes also the great passing over of which bodily death is only the sign. For man necessarily has to pass beyond the external and empirical level on which he first becomes aware of himself, and this constitutes a passage from death to life, if he accomplishes it successfully; but if he fails, he falls to a lower depth than before. This is the very lesson taught by the revelation of 'original sin'.

This passing over is not an optional matter. Lucifer himself could not avoid the dilemma: he had to be either the first of the Seraphim—or else Satan, the great Adversary.

Here again, he who flatters himself that he has reached the goal is in great danger of being lost, just as he who prides himself on his knowledge is in peril of knowing nothing. This point is expressed by the Upanishad in a series of rhythmical verses filled with paradox (9-14):

> Into utter darkness they depart
> who are attached to ignorance;
> but into darkness deeper still, it is said,
> go those who cling to knowledge.

Knowledge, no less than ignorance, must be transcended; the Īśa, like the Kena, never tires of repeating this—and it applies to every level of knowledge, from the most elementary to the most sublime. In all knowledge there is a danger of complacency and attachment, the temptation to halt on the way. God is beyond everything. Human thought can never discover more than the signs of his presence; but the impulse which the Spirit imparted to the creature in the first instant of its creation cannot be satisfied by anything less than the Real itself. A fitting commentary is given by the saying of Gregory the Great about the young Benedict when he lived as a hermit in his cave at Subiaco: "He was possessed of an ignorance which knew all, and a wisdom which knew nothing;" this is the same 'wise ignorance' of which the mediaeval mystics used to speak. In the last resort, God is found neither in knowledge nor in ignorance, for both consist simply of the concepts by which man seeks to represent him to himself. God simply *is* in himself. Truly man can say nothing about the 'passing over' to God. Is not this precisely that obscure and naked faith, of which John of the Cross sang in the *Dark Night of the Soul* (verse 3).

> In that gladsome night
> I secretly stood.
> By no one was I seen,
> and nothing did I perceive.

The Upanishad goes on to say:

> Knowledge has its place, and so has ignorance;
> this have we learnt from the men of old
> who distinguished them for us.
> When knowledge and ignorance
> both alike have been transcended,
> only then does a man pass to the further shore of death...
> and attains to immortality.

At last, having passed for ever beyond all darkness, he reaches that light of which the Muṇḍaka Upanishad says (2.2.9-10):

> In the sheath of gold is Brahman,
> pure, undivided; he is brilliant,
> the light of lights...
> In him the sun does not shine,
> nor the moon, nor the stars,
> nor does the lightning flash.
> He shines, and all things draw their light from him,
> in his light everything becomes luminous.

Verses 15 and 16 of the Iśa Upanishad are a fervent appeal to this 'light'. They are quoted from the Bṛhadāraṇyaka, and may originally have formed part of a funeral rite. In the form in which they have come down to us they apply just as well to the man who is facing the great

The Intuitions of the Rishis

'passing over' to the further shore of the self, of which physical death is the symbol at the level of the world of becoming:

> In the vessel of gold.
> is hidden the face of Truth.
> Open this vessel, O Pūṣan (Sun),
> so that I, who thirst for the Truth,
> may at last behold it!

or in an alternative rendering:

> The Real is hidden beneath a golden cup.
> O Pūṣan, unveil it for me,
> who am devoted to the Real,
> that I may see it!
> O Sun, send forth thy rays, withdraw thy glory,
> that I may behold the fairest form!
> Ah! he who is there on high, that Puruṣa—
> truly, it is I myself!

The vessel of gold which encloses and hides the face of Truth is surely the knowledge of creatures, and of God in creatures, to which man attains by his thought; and this knowledge is indeed a wonderful thing, bright with the glory which it spreads abroad. For the Upanishadic seers, the sun is the symbol of this glory which fills the world of 'manifestation' and is known by man in the reflection of it which he himself is in his spirit. And yet this 'face of glory, eludes us in the very moment of its self-manifestation. The face of glory, shown to us by the sun as it gives light to our world, is only the reflection of its true glory. It is the 'golden door', through which must pass those who are called to penetrate to the very heart of the Real, to the world of the supreme Brahman, the Immortal, Imperishable One (Muṇḍaka Up., 1.2.11).

Man cannot force an entrance here. The door opens only from within, but in its very opening all man's desires are at last fulfilled.

For the rishi one word, one phrase, was sufficient to fix and pass on his experience: in the Kena, Brahman—a lightning-flash; here, the sun which at once sends forth and draws back its rays. No more is required by one whose inner eye is open; to try to say more only profanes the mystery.

There is Being in itself, and Being as it manifests itself. There is God without a name, and God who is named from the signs through which he expresses himself. There is the Godhead, as Eckhart said, and there is the Trinity into which it unfolds. There is in any case—and this at least is in conformity with the strictest orthodoxy—God still unmanifested in the mystery of the Father, and God who expresses himself to himself in the Son, and who 'draws back' this Son to himself in the Spirit, so that the silence of the consummation rejoins that of the source.

There is also God in himself, and God who is manifested in creation, and in that slow maturation of creation which we call time. But in this creation and manifestation also, all returns at last to the Father. The Son comes forth from the bosom of the Father, but returns once more whence he came, in the glory of the Ascension.

In the case of the soul, the more fully it discovers God in the world of manifestation, the more irresistibly it is drawn towards what is beyond all manifestation. The Son does not allow anything to stop at himself, but bears all things to the Father, bringing everything to its consummation in the Spirit.

"O Sun, send forth and draw back thy rays, so that I who have come from thee, may at last find myself in thee, at the very heart of thy glory."

We may perhaps refer once more to St Benedict, who saw the whole world gathered up into a single ray of sunlight. As St Gregory comments, how could it be otherwise for one who contemplates the glory of the Creator?

The last line of verse 16 tells us of the final ecstasy of him upon whom the Glory has at last dawned, and who has discovered the mystery of his own being in the depths of that glory. He certainly could not have contemplated the glory face to face without being himself drawn deeply into it, as he finally awakes to himself in the ultimate truth of his being and in eternal non-duality with that glory.

Such expressions may sound strange to a Christian. And yet the mystery of the divine glory, *q*ᶜ*bod Yahweh*, is celebrated throughout the Bible. In particular, the texts of St Paul and St John, on which we were meditating side by side with these Upanishadic passages, helped us to glimpse the wonderfully prophetic Christian meaning in the words of the Iśa.

In his high-priestly prayer (John 17) the Lord asked his Father to bestow on his disciples that same glory which had been his even before the foundation of the world. Was not this the glory which was revealed on the Mount of Transfiguration? And was it not in the radiance of this same glory that John and Paul, for example. understood the profound meaning of the mystery of Christ's earthly life?

The Christian can never be satisfied until he has reached the very source of this glory, both beyond and within the sublimest forms of its manifestation. In the last analysis his prayer, his worship, his whole life, is no more than a heartfelt appeal to the Lord of Glory to reveal himself to his own in the mystery of his very being—as in the Transfiguration which is so dear to the piety of Eastern Christians; it is an ardent expectation of Christ's return in glory, as found in St Paul and the Acts; it is a still more hidden descent into the depths of his own heart, towards that glory which, according to St John, the preexistent Word had with his Father even before creation.

These words of verse 16 cannot, of course, be understood by the Christian in the same sense as they are by a Hindu jñānī, that is, to signify complete identity between the *Puruṣa*, the Person who is on high in the sun, at the heart of the glory of Being, and what he has hitherto called his own self. Nevertheless the Christian does experience something like this in the depths of his being, when in faith he hears the Father addressing to him the same call with which he eternally addresses his only Son, and finds welling up in his own soul the word uttered deep within him by the indwelling Spirit, the Son's eternal response to his Father: Abba, Father!

In this unity with the Son in the Spirit the Christian discovers at the same time his own new name (Rev. 2:17) and the name of God (3:12). Only in the Son does he have his being; it is only in the perfect Image which the Son is, that he himself is the image and likeness of God; it is only in the Person of the Son that he is loved by the Father and loves him in return. Only in the Son is he the reflection of the Glory of God. It is only in the Son, the unique *Puruṣa*, the unique Person, that whatever is capable of becoming conscious and awakening to itself actually does so. Only in the Son can a man become aware of himself in the truth, the reality and the immortality of his being.

The Christian's inexpressible discovery of himself in the glory of God is analogous to that of the Hindu jñānī at the moment of his disappearance in the glory of Brahman. And yet, for the Christian there still remains something beyond even this. His faith will at the last enable him to find himself again in God, in the mystery of his own personal vocation which is peculiar to himself and wholly incommunicable—eternally *one* with Christ and his brothers in the Father's presence, and yet distinct and for ever unique in that Father's love.

The penultimate verse of the Upanishad certainly belongs to the funeral rite referred to above:

> May the breath pass into the Wind,
> and the body to ashes!

This is a very timely reminder that the passage to glory, the transition to 'the further shore', or the 'great departure' (Kaṭha 1.29), necessarily entails a death, mystical no less than biological.

As for the last verse of the Īśa Upanishad, taken from the Rig-Veda (1.189.1), it would take very little to make it into a magnificent Christian prayer to the Spirit :

> Agni, lead us towards the Good,
> by way of a blessed path;
> Thou, the God who knowest all our works,
> Keep far from us the sin that leads astray.
> To thee for ever and ever
> Be offered the hymn of our praise!

The one whom the Self chooses

When we had finished reading the Kena and Īśa Upanishads, it was suggested that for the last Upanishadic meditation we should take a few verses from the end of the second chapter of the Kaṭha, of which the following is the most remarkable:

> The self cannot be attained by teaching,
> nor by understanding, nor by much learning;
> but the one whom the Self chooses,
> he alone attains the Self.
> To him the Self reveals his own (true) form (2.23).

This verse, like those quoted earlier from the Īśa represents the attainment of the Real as a grace. No human effort can achieve it. The hearing and study of the Scriptures are not enough by themselves. The Self alone freely reveals itself. As the masters of Vedānta explain, it reveals itself to itself and only to itself, shining with its own light. In this text of the Upanishad Ramaṇa Maharshi, for example, would therefore say that there is no question of grace, except from the point of view of one who still sees a duality. At the moment of awakening, you no doubt have the impression that another is snatching you away from yourself and drawing you to himself; but in reality—as you will discover in this very awakening—there never was a you plus *another*, a 'you' who have been taken out of yourself and 'another' who has carried you away. There never has been, is not now, and never will be anything but the unique One-without-a-second proclaimed by the Chāndogya Upanishad, or "that *Puruṣa* on high—who is myself" of the Īśa.

However, one should not weaken the very meaning of this verse of the Kaṭha by interpreting it in the light of quite different texts, which indeed might equally well be interpreted in their turn by it. In fact we frequently find in the Upanishads attempts to describe the supreme experience which seem, at least at first sight, mutually irreconcilable. The fundamental reason for this is the impossibility of expressing the total mystery of this experience in any human language whatever. The great advaitic statements (*mahāvākya*), which contain its essential core, are incapable of exhausting its richness. The rishis therefore now and then suggest other ways of expressing it, which the rational mind has great difficulty in harmonizing with the earlier statements.

A man may strive with all his power to attain to the supreme experience. He may persevere in practising the "Who am I?" of Ramaṇa Maharshi, or the "By whom is all this sent forth?" of the Kena Upanishad, he may apply himself to all the complications of yogic concentration; or, better still, he may produce within himself an emptiness of all thought and all desire, surrendering himself completely in total relaxation to the transcendent power whose presence he discerns within himself. But all this will fall short of the goal. The opening must be made from above or, if one prefers the expression, from the deepest centre of one's being. The 'golden door' is closed from the inside, and only from the inside can it be opened. It is necessary to be chosen, as the Upanishad says; and the Bible speaks no less emphatically of the effect of God's choice. "All that the Father gives me will come to me.." "I have manifested thy name to the men whom thou gavest me out of the world..." so says Jesus repeatedly in the Gospel (John 6:37; 17:6; etc). Often in the Psalms God is spoken of as the one who 'raises up', 'lifts up', 'receives' his people (*susceptor, suscipit*, in the Vulgate). To this raising or receiving by God corresponds man's 'receiving' or acceptance of his vocation; it was to "those who received him" that the Word gave the power to become the children of God (John 1:12).

This experience of *receiving* is characteristic of Christian faith and mysticism. It is this that enables us to penetrate into the infinite mystery of him who is "the God and Father of our Lord Jesus Christ" (1 Peter 1:3). The Christian knows that whatever he has, has been received by him as a free gift, as pure grace. He exists, but only in God and through the gift of God, which is the Spirit. He is immortal, but only by grace and in God, in the immortality of God, and not through any immortality of his own. He is a son of God, but only by grace, in the only Son, through the gift of God. All that he is, on the natural level as on the level of grace, he is by the communication, the gift of the Spirit.

This is possible precisely because there is already 'communication' in God, because God in himself *is* communion. In the inner life of communion which constitutes the very truth of Being, man becomes by grace what God is by nature; this is that 'divinization' (*theo-poiesis, dei-ficatio*), which was such a favourite theme of the Greek Fathers.

The being of man is wholly gift, wholly grace, wholly love. Even the revelation of sin, the manifestation of its dire presence at the heart of the individual, was essentially intended to enable man to realize this truth even more profoundly, and to show him that it is not merely from his 'nothingness', but from a radical unworthiness to exist, that God has 'raised him up' to himself.

In the last resort it is impossible to find any foothold or standing-ground apart from the gift itself as a basis from which to acknowledge the Giver or to offer him thanks and worship. Indeed, to tell God that we are offering him what he himself has given us smacks of artificiality. My very act of offering is his gift, as also are my gratitude and my adoration. Here again inescapably, it is a case of non-duality, the indivisible unity of the Spirit, *advaita, ekatvam;* I exist, but only within and at the heart of an act of giving, the very act in which God gives himself to me.

The wheel has come full circle, and the silence of the Christian mystic becomes one with that of the Upanishadic seer; but in the mean time the *kevala,* the aloneness of the Vedāntin, has been enriched with a communion.

6
THE JOHANNINE UPANISHADS

THE two final readings from the Bible were taken from St John. They formed a fitting conclusion and climax of all that we had so far read and pondered, either from the Bible or from the Upanishads. On Friday we read the Prologue and on Saturday morning, before separating, the great prayer of chapter 17, which concludes the farewell discourse.

That mystery which had first been glimpsed by the rishis is now revealed by St John in all its splendour, seen in the clear light of the Word and in the depth of the Spirit.

The Biblical texts studied hitherto had been chosen chiefly as a preparation for the Christian reading of the Upanishads, in order to remind us of the presence of the Spirit at the source of their message and to help us to recognize him there.

Our reading of the passages of St John was altogether different. It was as though we had returned from the Upanishads to the Bible with eyes miraculously unsealed, with eyes accustomed to the depths, capable of a wholly new penetration into the mystery of the Lord—perhaps something like what would happen if a Hindu, whose mind had been formed by long years of reading his own Scriptures and meditating on the inner mystery, were to read the Gospel in the light of his own experience of the ātman. There was, of course, no question—and this has to be constantly repeated to avoid misunderstanding—of finding in the Bible some new and fuller meaning of which the author himself was unaware. We found in St John simply what the Lord himself had put there; but we were also aware that there are always new discoveries to be made in Scripture, and it is precisely in order to help us to penetrate more deeply into the mystery of his Word that God has brought into being the rich variety of men and cultures.

The Logos Life and Light

In the Johannine Prologue we have a true Christian parallel to the 'soundings' or 'probes' into the mystery of being which we found in the Upanishads.

It has already been noted that the word *upanisad* originally signified those correspondences and interrelationships between the different levels of existence—those of the physical elements, of man's psychic or mental powers (the devas) and of the ātman—in which the ancient thinkers of India took such delight. The parallels are sometimes strained, but they are often extremely suggestive. By a whole series of successive approaches and a very subtle interplay of identifications which fit into each other like a nest of boxes, they lead unerringly to the perception of the Real itself. Tradition has singled out certain fundamental identifications, the *mahāvākya*, or "great utterances". These supreme *upaniṣads* epitomize Vedantic teaching in a particularly striking way. They include the identification of ātman and Brahman (*ayam ātma Brahma*, Maṇḍūkya 2), of I and Brahman (*aham Brahma asmi*, Brihadāraṇyaka 1.4.10) and of That and Thou (*tat tvam asi*, Chāndogya 6.8.6). These mantras, more than any others, contain and authentically sum up the essence of the Upanishadic experience; however, their truth can never be recognized in its fullness except by one who has 'realized himself' in that same experience. Used without discrimination at the conceptual level and in a purely intellectual way, they can lead to fatal aberrations.

More than any other passage in the Christian Scriptures, St John's Prologue recalls the Upanishadic approach, first in its use of the method of successive identifications, and then in its ever more profound penetration by this means into the mystery of God. This is surely a proof of the unity of the human spirit, underlying the differences of culture and intellect, which is manifested whenever it transcends those particular conditions which constrict and limit it, and in realizing its true self simultaneously discovers the very mystery of God, its Source. It is also a proof that the Spirit is there in every man, in the 'cave of the heart', waiting for the moment when he is at last ready, sufficiently silent to hear his voice and sufficiently free to yield to his influence.

We did not find in the Prologue, any more than in the Upanishads, a series of statements deduced one from another according to the laws of classical logic. It consists rather of a succession of intuitions, each of which leads on the next by some mysterious inner connection beyond the reach of conceptual logic, a sequence of piercing insights which draw us ever more deeply into the divine Abyss. By a strange paradox the Evangelist, who begins from God, and progressively descends to the level of the creature, discovers in each fresh intuition what seem to be further depths in the mystery of God.

The Johannine Upanishads

The rishis were seeking the foundation and ultimate principle of things, first in man and his consciousness, then in every being revealed to them by their senses, and finally in the cosmos as a whole. The problem which then confronted them was the ultimate non-duality of these apparently diverse principles, each of which seemed to be most fundamental in its own order.

John began from something given—the Living God, who had made himself known to John's own ancestors and to whom Jesus had borne witness in a wholly unique way. There was also the mystery of this world, as the creation and manifestation of God. There was finally the man whose life he had shared, whom he had seen, touched and listened to, and who had said that he was the Son of God. In the tradition of the prophets and sages of his people, the apostle had meditated profoundly on all that God had said of himself in the inspired books. His spirit was touched at an even greater depth by the words spoken by Jesus. All this had gradually taken complete possession of the Apostle's soul under the action of the Holy Spirit dwelling within him, until it became a living and incandescent personal experience. Then one day by the inspiration of this same Spirit, words welled up from the very heart of that experience which at last seemed capable of expressing his secret and introducing his brethren in their turn to the experience of the living God. And so, for the sake of the Church, John began to dictate.

John starts from the Logos, the Word, *debar Yahweh,* in which God had continually revealed himself to his people ever since the day when he chose to establish his Covenant with Abraham. It was in this Word that he had created all things in the beginning: "He commanded and they were created" (Ps. 148:5). Prophets and psalmists sang of the power of this word, and sages meditated deeply on its mystery, naming it Wisdom. The Greek term *logos,* which John chose to express the meaning of *debar Yehweh,* brought with it one of the most characteristic themes of contemporary Hellenistic wisdom. It signified the order and principle of the cosmos, the Reason which underlies and is at the heart of all things, and explains them all. Thus on the one hand we have the world as it was seen by the Jews in the light of divine revelation, created and kept in being by the word of God, and on the other, the world as understood by the Greeks in the light of reason, existing and developing according to its own immanent principles. All this is fused together in the mystery of the Logos, of whose glory John now sets out to sing:

> In the beginning was the Word;
> the Word was with God,
> and the Word was God,

'was God'; the expression he uses is not *theios*, divine, not *ho theos*, 'the' God, the Unique; but *theos* without the article, God who is called by the same name as the Unique, and yet is other than the Unique.

In John's thought, then, the Logos seems to be in the last resort the very principle of all that is and all that lives, being at once interior to and distinct from everything, the 'That' of which the rishis had an intuition and into whose mystery they entered by contemplation, naming it ātman and brahman, the self and the absolute.

This principle is at the heart of God, in the heart of him who made himself known to Moses as He-Who-Is and all through Israel's history continued to reveal himself as the Living God. And this Principle at the heart of God is himself God.

Next the Logos is identified with Life:

> Through him all things came to be,
> and not a single thing had its being except through him.
> All that came to be had life in him,
> and that life was the light of men,
> a light that shines in the dark....
> that enlightens every man who comes into the world.

Finally this Logos who is God, Life and Light, is identified with a man who was born upon earth and lived there like any other man, whom anyone was free to see, hear or touch, as he pleased (1 John 1:1):

> The Word (who had made all things)
> was made flesh
> and lived among us,
> full of grace and truth.

To all who receive him, all who receive the Life and the Light, the Logos gives the right to pass through the 'golden door', to have access to the heart of the divine mystery, to become sons in the only Son, and to behold his glory, the glory of the unique Son, for there is but a single Glory.

For the believer all that was said in the Upanishads was in reality said of Christ. But in the clear light of the Gospels all apparent contradictions are resolved. Within the glory of the One, the believer, his eyes unsealed by faith, perceives the Son who eternally proceeds from that One, and in the Son he beholds himself, in his own unique and irreplaceable vocation.

In St John we find not only the same method of approach, but also the same fundamental themes which were pondered by the Upanishadic sages. Of course, they are not precisely identical. The preparations for the Gospel were manifold; the abundant creativity of God has no need to repeat itself. But the similarities no less than the silences, the parallels which echo but do not repeat each other, compose the *līlā* of divine Providence "at play everywhere in his world" (Prov.8 :31), revealing to us in ever more wonderful ways the many facets of his mystery.

Thus, in the Prologue John identifies Light, whose praise is sung in the Īśa and Muṇḍaka Upanishads, with Jesus, and thereby introduces one of the most frequently recurring themes of his Gospel.

It is the same with Truth, *satyam*, the goal of all the Upanishads. At the end of the Prologue John presents the Word made flesh as "full of truth", the fullness of Truth, in other words Truth itself, as Jesus himself proclaims in chapter 14.

So too with Life, the immortality or 'non-death'. of the Upanishads. Jesus is the Life and the Way to eternal life, the bridge by which man crosses over to non-death. He himself is the immortality which the sages identified with the supreme knowledge.

We may truly say that Jesus is the Fullness which inspired the wonderful opening hymn of the Īśa.

Vāc, speech, the closest Sanskrit equivalent of *dābār* and Word, was also meditated on by the sages, though it was not given the same importance as the other themes that have been mentioned. It is rather OM, the *praṇava*, which scarcely occurs in our texts, that forms a closer point of contact. OM is the as yet undifferentiated sound in which God utters all that he utters, the beginning of his self-manifestation. OM is also the undifferentiated sound which ends in the silence in which all that man says about God, and all that God's manifestation' reveals about him, comes to fulfilment. Everything comes from God in his Word; and it is in the Word that everything returns to him. The Word is truly the original and ultimate OM, the first sound in which God utters himself and so utters all things, and the last word which sums up all that his creation has sought to express of him, so that the End unites with the Beginning "OM is all that was, all that is, all that will be," says the Māṇḍūkya Upanishad; "and OM is also all that transcends the three times." But the one who fills all time as he fills all space is "he who was, and is, and is to come," he before whom "every knee shall bow, in heaven and on earth and under the earth" (Rev. 5:8; Phil. 2:10). There is none that fills all times and yet transcends all times, except the Word of God made flesh, Christ the Lord, who comes from eternity and goes to eternity, who lives by the same life in the bosom of the Father and in the midst of men, and is present in his risen glory at every moment and every place in the universe. In the OM which he utters eternally God, in knowing himself, knows every man; in the same OM man knows himself and knows God. St John has more to say in chapter 17 about this knowledge, which is finally identified with light and life.

Besides the Prologue of St John, the supreme Christian Upanishad, there are certain other texts of the New Testament which also express the ultimate mystery of man and of God, having been revealed by the Spirit through correspondences which the unaided human reason could never have discovered. For example, "God is love" (1 John 4:16), to which one should add St Paul's characteristic insight in his hymn to charity: "If I have not love, I am nothing" (1 Cor. 13:2), implying that *my* being also is nothing but love, that Being itself is love. A far cry from the 'transcendental properties' of God, defined by philosophers!

Again, there is the identification which recurs with impressive frequency in John's Gospel, when Jesus applies to himself the divine name that was revealed on Horeb: *I am*. This is not only the *aham Brahma asmi*, "I am Brahman", but simply "I am", with no attribute so that the "I" is identified with Being (cp. John 8: 24, 28. 58, etc).

One might also quote the Eucharistic 'upanishad', "This is my body"—an identification which is not discovered in the mysteries of nature, but one realized by the power of the sacramental word. Paul explained later on that the Lord's body is also the Church, his *pleroma* or Fullness (cp. 1 Cor. 10:17; Eph. 1:23; Col 1:24). Moreover the demonstrative pronoun 'this' is very close to the *tad*, the 'that' of the Upanishad. Without insisting on the point, but rather by way of indicating starting-points for research one might recall that the *pleroma* of Christ is to embrace the whole of creation, the *sarvam idam* ("all this world") of the Iśa Upanishad, at least according to the plan of its Creator. On the other hand, the whole of the divine mystery, the *tad* of the same Upanishad, dwells in its fullness in the body of Christ, *somatikōs* (Col. 2:9). Truly the 'body' of Christ is a great mystery, whose eschatological fullness is sacramentally anticipated in the Eucharist.

In conclusion, we may note that extraordinary 'upanishad' of the Spirit which Paul throws out almost casually in the middle of his argument as if it was a fact whose truth was perfectly obvious; "Anyone who is joined to the Lord is one spirit with him" (1 Cor. 6:17). This identification is better understood in the light of Romans, chapter 8, where he explains that the mysterious *pneuma* (Spirit) dwelling within our own *pneuma* (spirit) moves us from the depths of our being and causes to spring up from our inmost hearts that very word "Abba" in which the Son expresses himself and returns to the Father.

There is no longer any question here of using the Bible as a preparation for reading the Upanishads and other texts of the spiritual and mystical tradition of India. What we must do is to make use of all that we have gained from our study of those texts in order to enter into a deeper and more experimental knowledge of our own Scriptures. For the Christian the Bible must always be the point of departure and the point of return; it is not a mere reference book, to be consulted now and then simply to illuminate or confirm the discoveries of reason or spiritual experience. It is from the Bible, God's self-revelation by his Word, his own Utterance, that all Christian experience takes off in its flight towards the infinity of God; it is also in the Bible alone that the Christian will find his own most authentic forms of utterance, when he attempts to express in his turn the mystery into which he has been introduced. Between these two poles lies the domain of the human mind, which also comes from God and goes to God, and whose whole development here below should be at the service of faith, the knowledge which obtains eternal life.

When we return to the study of the Bible after reading the Upanishads, we should not expect to find in it the selfsame concepts that they contain, even though, as we saw in the Prologue of St John, there are parallels which are truly overwhelming. The advaitic experience is no doubt timeless, but its formulation, even in the simplest Upanishadic expressions, always bears the mark of an age and a mental climate which are very different from those of the Bible. In addition, although the *mahavakya* or 'great utterances' quoted above are immensely evocative, the words in which Jesus communicates his experience of the Father and those in which his disciples have passed on their experience of God in Christ are incomparably more so; for they lead directly into the holy of holies, the mystery of God's communion with himself at the heart of his being.

Faith has enabled us to discover in the very depth of the Upanishadic experience of identity a reciprocity and a communion of love which, far from contradicting the *ekatvam*, the unity and non-duality of being, is its very foundation and *raison d'être*. However there can be no better introduction into the mystery of the unity of the Spirit than the advaitic experience of the *ekatvam* of being.

The Advaita of the Spirit

The seventeenth chapter of St John, to an even greater extent perhaps than the Prologue, helps us to understand how in the perspective of Christian faith the Bible can be seen without exaggeration as the crown and completion of the Upanishads.

In this passage we find, expressed now in Biblical terms, the boldest and most challenging of the Upanishadic discoveries. The language is certainly different, but the profound experience it seeks to convey is the same—or rather, the experience of the Upanishads is here seemingly put to the test and reaffirmed in the light of Christ.

We shall now see what St John says to us in this chapter, or rather, what Jesus himself teaches us of the ultimate mystery; for we have here the very words of Christ as John heard them, not merely with his bodily ears, but with all the attention of his 'listening heart', as he rested blissfully upon the Lord's breast.

The Son has received from the Father, in the very act of divine generation, all that the Father himself possesses. The Father has nothing which does not also belong to the Son in virtue of his divine nature. This follows necessarily from their being 'consubstantial' (*homoousios*), as was defined by the Council of Nicea.

And all this—all that he is, all that he has received from the Father—is communicated by Jesus to his disciples. This is not merely a piece of theological or gnostic fantasy; it is a truth to which John himself, the beloved disciple, bears witness, for he heard it from the very lips of Jesus. All that Jesus has by nature, he has shared with his own by grace. He has given them everything, keeping back nothing for himself; he communicated to his apostles the secrets of the divine life which in eternity he hears from the Father, so that they in their turn might share them with the gtenerations of Christians to come:

> Father, I have given them

The Johannine Upanishads

> the words which thou gavest me... (17:8)
> I have given them thy word... (17:14)
> I have called you *friends,*
> for *all* that I have heard from my Father
> I have made known to you (15:15).

In another chapter of this Gospel, Jesus compares the knowledge with which he knows his own and that with which they know him to his knowledge of the Father and the Father's knowledge of him:

> I know my own
> and my own know me,
> as the Father knows me
> and I know the Father (10:14-15).

This is surely that secret knowledge, revealed only to the 'babes', of which Jesus speaks in the hymn of exultation, uttered when his heart was filled with wonder and gratitude towards the Father (Matt. 11:25ff):

> No one knows the Son except the Father,
> and no one knows the Father except the Son
> and anyone to whom the Son chooses to reveal him.

This is the knowledge in which the Father begets the Son and in which the Son receives the very being of the Father; it is the 'revelation' of God first of all within his own being, and then that which the Son has come to manifest to the world, inviting all those who receive this 'revelation' (which he himself is) to become partakers in his divine Sonship (John 1:12, 18).

As the Father and the Son are *one,* so the Son and all who are his are *one,* all of them united with him:

> May they all be *one;*
> even as thou, Father, art in me, and I in thee,
> that they also may be in us... (17:21)
> that they may be *one,* even as we are *one...* (17:22)

one with that unity of which Jesus says elsewhere:

> the Father and I are one (10:30).

The Glory which the Father has given to his Christ, that which the Lord receives from the Father as his only Son, which is his from the beginning, before ever the world was (17:5), and which is to be mysteriously bestowed on him anew in his Passion—this same Glory has been given also to his own "that they may be one", for it is only in this Glory that there is unity, *ekatvam:* "The glory which thou hast given me I have given to them" (17:22).

"I desire that they also...may behold my glory"—so the Lord prays (17:24); "we have beheld his glory," testifies St John (1:14).

Man cannot contemplate the Glory without being engulfed in it. Jesus reveals nothing that he does not also give. The knowledge of that Glory is itself eternal Life (17:3). Just as there can be only one Glory, so there can be only one Life—that which from the beginning was in the bosom of the Father, and in which all that came to be is life (1:4).

So too Jesus communicates in all its fullness the Joy which is his—"that they may have my joy fulfilled in themselves" (17:13); "that my joy may be in you, and that your joy may be full" (15:11)—God's own joy, the Joy which is God himself, which is promised to the faithful servant, "Enter into the joy of your Lord" (Matt. 25:21).

He also reveals to them the Name of the Father, that Name which he alone is able to know and utter, since he alone, in virtue of his eternal birth, dwells in the Father's heart: "I have made known to them thy name" (17:26). To reveal the Name—the Name which Yahweh refused to tell to Jacob (Gen. 32:29), and of which his angel said to Gideon that it is "wonderful, mysterious" (Judges 13:18)—is to reveal the Person, to admit to the most intimate secret of his being, to open the way to his heart.

Lastly, Jesus communicates to us without reserve the Love with which he is loved by the Father and with which he loves him in retrun:

> As the Father has loved me,
> so have I loved you;
> abide in my love (15:9).
> ...that the love with which thou hast loved me
> may be in them (17:26).

All this is included in the gift of the Spirit, who is the indivisible love of the Father and the Son.

As there is only one Father, there is only one Son and one unique Knowledge, that which the Father has of the Son and the Son of the Father.

As there is only one Son, there is only one Spirit, one Gift, one Love—the Gift, that is, the mutual exchange and the gaze wholly fixed on the *Other* which the Father is for the Son and the Son for the Father, the Love, that unique Love, with which Father and Son love each other eternally.

Creation adds nothing to God, to Being. Nothing that is can ever be anything but a manifestation of God, a manifestation that occurs within the very depths of God. Nothing can be called into being which does not have its being in the Son. Nothing can be called into awareness of being, except in the knowledge which the Son has of the Father; and nothing can be called to love, joy or glory, except in the one Spirit who is the Fullness of God.

What the Upanishads and the Hindu tradition express in terms of Being, the Christian Scriptures, in accordance with the peculiar genius of the Semitic languages, present to us in terms of Life, Knowledge of the Name, Love, Joy and Glory. This revelation is no less overwhelming to human reason than the other, for reason is unwilling to admit that God is beyond its grasp, and that his works and the outpouring of his love cannot be confined in the concepts that it freely constructs—and this, alas, often even after it has been enlightened by faith...

And yet, could God really have acted differently? Could be have given us anything less without being unfaithful to his promise and falling short of his faithfulness and truth, so often mentioned in the Psalms?

In the Epistle to the Romans St Paul tells us that we are fellow-heirs of Christ and heirs of God (8:17). If truly we are his sons—and God is Truth, and the truth of what he says stands for ever—then surely there can be nothing in the kingdom of our Father which is not ours. Would anyone dare to accusē God of not taking seriously the name and status of *sons,* which he has given us and which Jesus came to reveal and make a reality in us? God does not trifle with us, even if our understanding is too weak to fathom the wonders of his wisdom and love (Rom. 11:33; Eph. 3:19).

In the last resort it is in the light of such texts that the whole Gospel of St John, and indeed the whole New Testament, should be read. Again and again we meet echoes of the same themes, as for example:

> We shall see him as he really is (1 John 3:2).
> Now we are seeing a dim reflection in a mirror;
> but then we shall be seeing face to face.
> The knowledge that I have now is imperfect;
> but then I shall know as fully as I am known (1 Cor. 13:12).

In the depths of his inner silence, as though issuing from the primordial OM, the Indian sage hears the murmur of *saccidānanda* (*sat-cit-ānanda*)—"being, awareness of being, infinite joy"—the expression, still very obscure, of his unutterable experience.

In the depths of the silence of the Spirit, as though issuing from the indwelling Word, the Christian, who meditates on this chapter of St John, cannot help hearing deep within himself this same *sat-cit-ānanda*, which has now yielded up its secret:

> Thou art one with me,
> as I myself am One with the Father
> in the infinite Glory of Being—

the supreme revelation of *SAT,* Being one and undivided;

> having received from me
> that same knowledge
> which I have of him—

the revelation of *CIT,* God's own Awareness that *He is;*

> loved by him and loving him,
> as he and I love each other
> in the very fullness of our Bliss—

the supreme revelation of *ANANDA,* the Bliss of Being.

This is the Christian Saccidānanda—all awareness, all communion. It is the Spirit's own mystery, the ultimate secret of God, in the depths of the Father's heart.

According to the Christian faith, there is a double 'procession' in God, that of the Word, and that of the Spirit.

In the procession of the Son, it is what may be called God's *otherness* that is revealed, his knowledge and awareness of himself, his self-communication within his own Self.

In the procession of the Spirit, on the other hand, it is God's unity that is revealed and comes to expression, the Communion of the *One* with the *Other,* the mutual coinherence of the Father and the Son.

The first procession is a manifestation. The second, beyond all manifestation, so to speak, attains to that in God which is not and never could be manifested. The Spirit can never be grasped and is always referred to in Scripture under symbols of what is fleeting and mobile.

In the procession of the Son, God gives himself a name and makes himself known. In the second, he reveals himself as unknowable.

The first procession is the existential foundation of everything that appears manifold in this world. The second reveals in everything the mystery of *ekatvam*, unity, non-duality.

The first is the Son's cry of Abba, Father. The second is the OM which ends in silence.

And it is this double mystery, the very mystery of Being, which from the deepest recesses of his own consciousness, recalls man to himself—

> to Being,
> to Awareness of being,
> to the infinite Bliss of being,
> SACCIDĀNANDA!

Some theologians would no doubt wish to belittle the importance of the Gospel texts that we have been studying. Similarly there are Hindu exegetes who attempt to confine the Upanishadic intuitions within mental concepts which they confuse with the experience of God.

It would certainly be rash to interpret the intuitions of the apostles as though they were Aristotelian definitions. They overflow on every side the words in which they were formulated. Here it is essential to remember that theology is something totally different from philosophical speculation on the data of revelation. Theology is fundamentally a *logos* concerning God. Now the Logos is *theos;* he is in God and he is God. It is only within God himself that we can hear the Logos which God says of himself and in which he says all.

Does this not prove once more that it is only in 'the cave of the heart', the depths of the spirit to which the Upanishads bring us, that man can begin to 'understand' what it means to be one in unity with other men, to be individual beings and yet all one with the Lord, to be, in the Lord, one with the Father, the Source and Consummation of all things, in the non-dual mystery of the unique Spirit, in the unity (*ekatvam*) of the Holy Spirit?

It remains true, however, that the Biblical revelation is given to us as we are, men living in time. Jesus did not intend to withdraw us from time, but only from the bondage of time, from everything in it that must die, that 'passes away and does not return', from the limitation, instability and illusion that is inherent in time, so long as its eschatological meaning has not been perceived. The summons to eternity comes to us in the very midst of our temporal existence, and the epiphany* of the Lord penetrates our phenomenal consciousness to the extreme limits of its involvement in matter and in time.

Vedantic writers have speculated endlessly on the notions of *māyā* (illusion) and *līlā* (the divine 'sport'), and too often the commentators have spoken of the world of *māyā* and *līlā* as a kind of substitute for being, without realizing that in so doing they were denying the reality of the Absolute.

The Christian revelation, on the other hand, takes the whole epiphany of God with the utmost seriousness; first, the manifestation which takes place at the heart of the Absolute, the double communication in which Being has its origin and comes to its consummation; and again that even more mysterious manifestation in the abyss of his love, in which his creation simultaneously springs from and returns to him, at the heart of Being.

Nothing exists which is not ātman, declares the Iśa Upanishad. There is nothing that is not within the ātman, whether it be the minutest particle of matter, or the briefest moment of time. It is precisely this truth that Jesus revealed to us by incarnating himself, 'true God of true God', in a genuinely human body and soul. In so doing he consecrated the whole of matter, space and time, for there is nothing in the universe which is not bound up with and in communion with the totality.

Jesus revealed the Father as the source and term of the cosmos; he himself came from the Father 'in the fullness of time' to redeem time and bring it to its completion; he manifested the divine fullness in the midst of the world of space and time, and in his very return from the midst of time to his Father, he continues to be present to every moment of time through his meta-temporal existence as the Risen one. And thus he has provided at last the solution of the paradox of advaita, which was sought for so long by the Vedantic thinkers, and which even the jñānīs who sensed it intuitively were unable to express in formal concepts.

At this point, however, the Western Christian would be extremely ill-advised to confront the Vedantic sage with the conventional dualist categories of his own philosophy, and still less to offer him a so-called

---

*epiphany—the showing, manifestation, of the divine glory in the created world and in time.

Christian Advaita, in which he would be unable to recognize anything of his own supreme experience.

Certainly there can be no question of relegating, for example, the whole history of salvation to some imagined transcendent sphere, after the fashion of Valentinus and the Gnostics, for this would be to deny both Vedānta and Christianity. On the contrary, we must recognize the mystery of the Presence—indivisible, eternal, non-dual—at every stage of the mystery of salvation and in its consummation; for salvation extends throughout the universe, from beginning to end, redeeming it and drawing it back from nothingness.

The Paschal mystery of Redemption was accomplished at a definite time and place in the cosmos. But in reality, Redemption is neither something past nor something yet to come. It is wholly and entirely realized in this present moment, in which I actually am. It is now, in this instant of my existence and of my presence to myself, conditioned as it is by all the providential circumstances which have prepared for it, that the Spirit in the depths of my heart murmurs "Abba", the response of the sons of God. And it is also in this moment that I "pass from non-being to being," from time to eternity,

> crossing to the further shore of death,
> and attaining to Immortality, beyond the darkness.

However, this image is still quite inadequate, for the passage from non-being to being, from time to eternity, is but a symbol of my complete freedom in the acceptance of being, a token of my power to accept or refuse being and immortality. It is always possible for being to fail to develop in me; I can become one of those 'slayers of the self' of which the Īśa Upanishad speaks.

In the last resort, the Paschal mystery is the realization in me of my awakening to being, which takes place at the very well-spring of being. I am so deeply immersed in the mystery of God himself that it is within the very act by which God calls himself into being that I myself am.

The paradoxes which Master Eckhart employed to make this clear delighted the holy women who heard him, and for them all his words were but fleeting pointers to be quickly left behind. The theologians, however raised their eyebrows, and were not wholly at fault in warning simple folk against the soaring flights of the Master. Some of these, like the formulations of the Upanishads, were wonderful in themselves and pregnant with the highest truth, but at the same time extremely dangerous for anyone who listened to them at a spiritual level other than that on which they were originally uttered.

The Father calls the Son, and in that same call the Son responds to the Father. In that mysterious exchange is included the summons to the creature and its response in time—Abraham's "Here am I" and Mary's "Behold, the handmaid of the Lord"—a response which rises up to God 'out of the depths' of non-being and of sin.

In thus responding, the creature attains to the being that it will have for all eternity, for in this very act it comes to personal existence and to freedom; and is this not a sharing in the awakening of Being to itself at the dawn of eternity? Is not the act of faith by which a man is justified and the love which animates that act of faith truly a 'theandric' act in which both man and God are indissolubly involved? It is a free and spontaneous response to God, and at the same time pure grace, pure gift of God, pure activity of the Spirit in man. Who can possibly separate out and distinguish what is of God and what is of man in this essentially non-dual act in which I attain to God, attain to Being, and awake to myself in the heart of God's own awakening to himself?

It is fatal mistake to conceive of eternity as a kind of limitless time, or to speak of it in terms derived from time. The eternal present of God fills every moment of my own present. It is meaningless to say that God was 'before' me. If the Bible occasionally makes use of such expressions, that is simply out of consideration for our weakness, in order to wean us gradually from the 'milk of babes' until we are ready for solid food (cp. Heb. 5:12).

Within the divine mystery, the awakening of the Father to being is only dialectically distinguished from the awakening of the Son. The awakening is *homo-ousios*, 'of one substance', non-dual—once again *advaita*. In the Son's awakening the whole of creation awakes to being, at the dawn of eternity of which the Easter dawn is the manifestation in time.

The Scriptures and traditions of India are certainly a wonderful help to the Christian in realizing and experiencing in its fullness the essential non-duality of the Paschal mystery. For if a man has never experienced the non-duality of being, and never been carried beyond the limits of his understanding, beyond all that he has felt, thought or known about himself, into his source in the unfathomable depths of being, he runs a grave risk of understanding very little of the secret of love and eternal life which Jesus revealed—"very little of what he is of God, very little of what is of God in all things," to repeat the phrase of the Kena Upanishad.

As long as he looks upon God as 'another' in the sense in which his neighbour is 'other' to him, as long as for him Jesus too is 'another', and he sees the divine Persons also as 'other' both to him and among themselves, he has not begun to understand anything either of himself or of God. The ultimate mystery lies at the very heart of non-duality. Only the Spirit of unity can silently teach this mutual gaze of love in the depths of Being, of which all earthly 'otherness' is simply the sign.

There is in fact only one upanishad, the one revealed by Jesus. The disciple who during the Last Supper lay close to the Saviour's breast understood in that communion of love all that the rishis of India had learnt of the non-duality of being in the depth of their inner solitude.

The Indian sages, starting out from their everyday experience of the world of the senses and of thought, and ascending by means of a progressive series of subtle correspondences through ever higher levels of being, at last in their own inner depths reached the transforming experience of bliss. John, the beloved disciple, pondering on what he read of God in the Old Testament and what he heard from the lips of Jesus, and always attentive to the Spirit speaking in his heart, at last understood and revealed to the Church the truth he had learnt: the glory of the Unique is the same glory as was manifested in the face of Jesus and witnessed by his apostles, and the same glory that was revealed by grace in the depths of their own hearts; the Love of the Unique is the same as the love with which Jesus had loved them and which also welled up, like a spring of living water, in their own hearts; the "I" that Jesus uttered is the "I" of the Unique: and within the same unity which made him one with the Unique, they too were one with each other and with him, for in him they come from the Father and return to the Father, in the advaita of the Spirit.

7
SOME PROBLEMS DISCUSSED

BEFORE we came together at Nagpur it had been very clearly stated that we intended to remain strictly on the level of 'contemplative meditation', and that purely speculative discussions would be carefully avoided. The subject-matter of our conversations should not be mere theories with little bearing on reality, but concrete experiences and truly existential problems.

Alas, the demon of argument is perhaps the most difficult of all to exorcize! And perhaps it is even more difficult to bring a man to realize that he is entering on a path on which he has himself declared that no one should set foot. So it happened that the exchange of thoughts on the passage from the Katha Upanishad mentioned above quickly developed into an extremely academic comparison of Christian mysticism and its Hindu counterpart. This discussion moreover did justice neither to the Christian faith-experience nor to the experience of Vedanta. The experience of the non-duality of being in no more susceptible of clear definition than the Christian experience of transforming union. The first fervours and aridities of the novice are not to be identified with the 'prayer' of quiet' and the 'dark nights'. No more can the Vedantic experience be reduced either to the conceptual vacuum or the sensation of 'cosmic expansion' which beginners in yoga sometimes meet with in their attempts at concentration.

A Challenge

This probably explains the rather violent reaction of one who was present as a guest-member of the group. He considered that we were not taking sufficiently seriously the problem, if not the challenge, presented to Christianity by advaita when it is genuinely experienced and lived. In his view our discussions too quickly became a facile refutation of advaita in the name of a Christian theology which had not even examined its own basis, and was moreover content with mere shadow-boxing against a purely imaginary concept of Advaita of its own invention.

In the same way it sometimes happens that Hindus extract from the Gospels a picture of Christ formed by their own personal ideas and experience. They are so sure of their conclusions that they naively criticize Christians for finding anything in the Gospel that does not conform to their own interpretations of Vedanta! We have to admit, however, that the Christian runs an equal risk of constructing for his own use a Christian version of Advaita which excludes on principle anything that does not fit into a previously determined framework—and this, even before he has made any attempt to enter into the advaitic experience from within. So our friend relentlessly brought us back to the absolute claims of Vedānta. He would allow no one to rest content with an *a priori* refutation, or an equally superficial acceptance, of a given Upanishadic text, or more generally, of the whole advaitic tradition still living in India. He reminded us insistently of the contemporary example of Ramana Maharshi. Sometimes indeed he gave the impression that for him the experience of Śrī Ramaṇa was the norm by which all mystical experience should be judged in any spiritual or religious context whatever. He forgot, of course, that the experience of the sage of Arunachala was, like that of any other man, conditioned at least in its expression, and also that, according to the Indian proverb, "Only a jñānī can judge a jñānī." For who indeed would venture to pronounce judgement on that which, of its very nature, transcends all judgment?

His attitude inevitably provoked contrary reactions. However, the resulting tension was not harmful and did not in the least diminish the cordiality of our discussions. Above all it had the salutary effect of not allowing anyone to remain satisfied with his own sometimes too hasty generalizations.

Some of the participants felt obliged to defend the 'true' Christian faith, and to stress the incompatibilities between Vedantic formulations and statements of Christian dogma. Others thereupon reminded them that, however necessary such a comparison might be, it should be left for a later occasion. Our immediate aim was to penetrate as deeply as possible into the secret of the experience enshrined in the Upanishads, leaving aside all reference to anything else, and hoping in faith that the Spirit would himself bring about the desired 'osmosis'* in the depths

---

*osmosis—a metaphor derived from the tendency of certain fluids, when separated by a porous barrier, to pass through it and intermingle.

of our hearts thus laid open to his action. Only out of such an osmosis at the level of lived experience will it be possible later on for understanding to develop at the level of conceptual thought. However this understanding will never be brought about either by the confrontation of opposing ideas or by intellectual efforts to reach a synthesis; it will rather be the gradual and progressive discovery of a higher truth in the depths of the soul which remains alert and recollected in the Presence.

It seemed at times that some of us sensed a real danger of losing their faith through a too close contact with the Upanishads—as though a real and genuine faith could be so easily be lost! The answer given was that of Origen in the Preface to the *Contra Celsum:* "If I am really a Christian," says the great master in substance, quoting St Paul (Rom. 8:35ff), "who or what will ever be able to separate me from Christ? Tribulation, anguish, persecution, hunger, danger, the sword? How much less the jeers of Celsus!" No more, we may add, can the affirmations of the Upanishads, those 'heights and depths' of which Paul speaks a few lines further on. Surely everything comes under the royal power and headship of Christ, and all things are to find in him their end and fulfilment. There cannot therefore be any precious thing in the world, however hidden or strange, that is not already taken up, at least potentially, into his pleroma.

The real stumbling-block for Christianity does not lie in India's advaitic experience, but in the many 'monistic' expressions of that experience—and also in the 'dualistic' formulations which are frequently offered of the Christian faith. The latter indeed often mislead Hindus with regard to the true essence of Christianity, because they give them the impression that Christian experience remains at a hopelessly superficial level. In the West the chief reason for the failure of Christianity to stem the advance of Communism has been the fact that too many Christians have forgotten the Gospel of love and service proclaimed by Jesus at the beginning of his ministry. But here in India it is rather that they forget the spiritual Gospel with which he completed and crowned his teaching.

Advaita is not so much a challenge to Christian faith as a relentless reminder that God—and therefore also the acts of God—can never be wholly contained in our concepts. It is a healthy and permanently necessary reminder of the importance of the 'way of negation'. It condemns, and at the same time frees us from, the idolatry of the

Some problems discussed

intellect, in which our laziness and pride perpetually threaten to engulf us. It rejects the self-satisfied, characteristically bourgeois, reliance on institutions and rites which, however indispensable and sacramentally effective they may be, nevertheless are only signs. It delivers us from our very human tendency to transform the ineffable mystery of the Trinity into a kind of refined tritheism,* or at the other extreme, into simple modalism,* despite the theoretical orthodoxy of our credal statements. It also frees us from the temptation somehow to 'add up' God and ourselves, his creatures, on the grounds that we are not God—thus falling into a dualism no less contrary to the faith than monism.

All this constitutes a direct and inexorable attack on our congenital self-centredness. Of ourselves we quite naturally judge everything from our own angle. We project God in front of us, and imagine him after our own image. Even the revelation that he has given us of his mystery has to pass through this mental bottleneck. Everything is subordinated to the fundamental assertion of this self of mine—a self that is moreover perilously restricted to the merely bodily and mental levels. If Advaita appears to us as a threat, it is precisely because it will allow nothing to remain of that superficial bodily, or at best merely mental, ego which belongs to the level of concepts. It will never allow us to rest content with anything less than the "I" which God utters within himself, in the mysterious procession of the Word and Spirit. The challenge of Advaita is addressed not to Christianity, but to the laziness and pride of Christians. It condemns their reluctance to accept once and for all these words of Jesus: "Whoever seeks to gain his life will lose it, but whoever loses his life will preserve it" (Luke 17:33). He has told us the inexorable law that governs the entry into life: "In order to be fruitful, a seed must fall into the ground and die" (cp. John 12:24).

There is no real contradiction between Advaita and Christianity, but only between the false substitutes which usurp their place, the premature and inadequate syntheses put forward on both sides by those who imagine that experience can be confined within their definitions.

---

*tritheism, modalism—two opposite attempts (both unacceptable) to give a rational account of the Trinity; the former stressing the distinction of the Persons in such a way as to end in the affirmation of three Gods: the latter preserving the unity of God by reducing the Persons to mere 'modes' or aspects of the One.

Only the man who is ready to go to the end in the experience both of the Christian faith and of Advaita will find the solution to the apparent antimony. It is to be found in a higher light, which human reason alone will never be able fully to account for. Even when enlightened by faith and guided by Scripture and tradition, has man's reason ever been able to find an adequate expression of the mystery of grace, of God's concurrence in his own free action? The theologians who have attempted to do so have invariably got into difficulty by going to one or the other extreme, while mutually denouncing each other as heretics. In fact both sides have fallen victim to the same dualistic presupposition which assumes that God and man can be added together. But Advaita means precisely this: neither God alone, nor the creature alone, nor God plus the creature, but an indefinable non-duality which transcends at once all separation and all confusion.

The Kena Upanishad says truly that Indra, the intellect, is incapable of recognizing Brahman. It is only after Brahman has vanished into the 'space' of the spirit that there appears in that same space Umā the radiant and lofty wisdom which reveals to man the Mystery which had as it were touched him in the depths of his being. This is also the paradox of the Īsā Upanishad:

> He who clings to ignorance is lost;
> he who clings to knowledge is even more so!

As long as *vidyā* (knowledge) is regarded as an alternative to *avidyā* (ignorance), there is no knowledge, and the Truth is not yet attained.

Advaita is not opposed to anything—if it were, it would no longer be itself. In the same way, when Christianity sets itself over against any other religious tradition, as if it were itself 'another' religion, it thereby denies the transcendence which belongs to it by right, for transcendence admits of neither otherness nor comparison.

In everything that has any positive content of truth Christianity recognizes itself as potentially present, for, as Augustine says, Christ is already there. The Church too is already present everywhere, for the Church is simply Christ reaching out to all places and all times. The fact that she only becomes visible at particular times and in particular places does not affect her essential nature. There is nothing true, beautiful or good, which does not to bear the mark of the Spirit. Evil only emerges when what is true, beautiful or good stops short at itself, claiming to be the All, the final plentitude, and refuses the role in the

Some problems discussed

history of salvation which is the very purpose of its creation. This was the temptation of the cherub in the garden of Eden, described by Ezekiel:

> Your heart has grown swollen with pride
> on account of your beauty.
> You were once an exemplar of perfection,
> full of wisdom, perfect in beauty...
> You have corrupted your wisdom
> owing to your splendour (28:11-17).

One of the questions raised at Nagpur was just this: What would be the atittude of jñānī, if brought face to face with the reality of Christ?

It was pointed out that first of all one would have to take into account the circumstances of such a meeting. It should not be understood in terms of mere preaching of the kind that does not penetrate to the 'cave of the heart', where alone a message becomes truly personal. But if the message truly reaches that point and is recognized by the jñānī himself as an invitation issuing from the depths of his own being, then one can say with confidence that a true jñānī, one who had known the ultimate experience, could not reject it. For is not the jñānī by definition a pure openness to the Spirit, since he is wholly freed from all selfishness?

A *sinful* refusal of Christ—like that of Lucifer or the religious leaders who, according to St John, knew the truth but refused to submit to it—is inconceivable except in the case of a man who is still 'on the way'. He might then refuse the Lord in the name of an advaita of his own conceiving, one which only glorified his own ego and puffed him up with pride. Or it might happen in the case of one who was a jñānī or yogī only in appearance. In such an individual, far from his empirical self vanishing in the supreme Self, what has happened is that the ego of his phenomenal consciousness has taken to itself the supreme and absolute character of the "I" of the real Self. In fact, he has magnified himself after the fashion of the devas in the Kena Upanishad—a temptation which many unfortunately fail to resist.

One member of the group stressed the possibility that the message of Christ might well be the decisive sign and the means of discernment appointed by God to bring such a man to the ultimate realization. Still, at the depth of awareness and self-mastery to which his spiritual training has brought him—just before the opening of the 'golden door'—the freedom of a truly spiritual Hindu is such that his consent to adore, or his refusal to do so, will be made in total lucidity. This is the mystery of ultimate choices, of which Scripture speaks clearly.

Here someone objected that this is primarily an intellectual problem, and is irrelevant at the level of awareness at which the jñānī is established, for nothing can ever come into *dvandva*, or opposition, with the experience of the self. Conflicts of ideas and dilemmas of conscience only arise in the sphere of *nāma-rūpa*, that is, of the 'names and forms' of this world of manifestation, of phenomena. The spiritual eye of the jñānī pierces like a laser beam through all particular things, and discovers the unique splendour of Brahman shining in all of them. Thus he will intuitively see the Lord in all things and all things in the Lord. He will freely acknowledge the fullness of Christ's glory, but he will recognize the same fullness of glory as the birthright of every conscious being. He will regard all the formulations of the mystery of Christ proposed by Christian tradition, and especially that of his Paschal glory, as being magnificently heightened expressions of man's awakening to himself, "to the glory which was his even before the world was made"—because, for him who knows, this awakening is the fullness of being itself. Then, as Jesus knew himself to be free with regard to the Mosaic law, so the jñānī will realize that no law, no *dharma* is binding on him. Man, the *bar-nasha* (son of man) of the Gospel, is lord even of the Sabbath, and the sons of the Kingdom are utterly free. In fact, the problem is insoluble at the level on which we were discussing it; it can only be seen in its proper perspective by a realized man. Only one who in the depth of his experience of self-awareness has discovered the mystery of the Son and the Father has any right to judge the Hindu jñānī, for he alone can understand him.

Integration

There can be no question of dreaming about an impossible synthesis between Advaita and Christianity, or even of a 'Christian transcendence' of Advaita: for as soon as Advaita is given any qualification whatever, it ceases to be Advaita. Such forms of expression assume that Christianity and Advaita can confront each other as though they were separate realities. This may be true up to a point on the conceptual level, but it no longer holds on the real and existential level. Both Christianity and Advaita claim to be transcendent with regard to everything else. Moreover, to compare the formulations of Shankara with those of Denzinger and judge them accordingly would be as futile as to try to judge in terms of each other such differing expressions of the Christian faith as have been left to us by, for example, Thomas Aquinas and Duns Scotus.

In reality, advaita is already present at the root of Christian experience. It is simply the mystery that God and the world are *not two*. This mystery of unity, *ekatvam*, in God and in all the works of God, is personified by the Spirit. Before leaving his disciples, Jesus laid great stress on the mysterious presence of the Spirit in them. He entrusted them to the keeping of this Spirit. In her turn the Church recalls the Spirit and his mystery of unity in the conclusion of all her solemn prayers: "in the unity of the Holy Spirit." She also invokes him in the Eucharistic *epiclesis** and at the beginning of every sacramental blessing.

Instead of speaking of synthesis or transcendence, it would be much more accurate to speak of the advaitic dimension of revelation and of Christianity. This is also a dimension inherent in the act of faith which leads to salvation—we should perhaps call it a dimension of depth, of which contact with the Upanishadic experience makes one more fully aware.

If in fact Advaita did not lie at the very heart of a Christian's act of faith, it would follow that there had been two successive thrusts and two objectives in God's work: first of all, a plan at the level of pure nature, according to which man was to develop towards the perfection of his nature simply by the use of his own gifts and abilities; and later, the plan of the redemptive incarnation, involving a radical change of direction and imposing on man a completely new end. But this is wholly incompatible with Biblical and patristic tradition. Since its expulsion from Eden the human race has known throughout the course of history only two conditions: a state of fallen nature and a state of redeemed nature. Man's whole existence is ordained to salvation in and through Christ.

In the jñānī's acceptance of his condition at the moment of attaining to the supreme illumination, we may surely see the equivalent of the Christian's act of faith in Christ. Is it not kind of foreshadowing and antitype of the Paschal mystery? The transcendence of his empirical self and the attainment of the 'further shore' which is the ultimate sphere of his being, can surely be compared with the crossing of the

---

*Epiclesis (Greek)—call, invocation: in Christian liturgy, especially that of the Eastern Church, a prayer made to the Holy Spirit that his work may produce the sacramental effect, above all, the Eucharistic transformation.

Red Sea. His entry into the cloud which hides him from himself when he is immersed in the supreme Splendour, recalls Moses' ascent of the Mountain of God whose slopes were veiled in cloud while its summit blazed with fire. To reach this point, the jñānī has had to surrender himself completely, leaving behind all the efforts of his understanding to express after its own fashion the mystery of man and the mystery of God. It is in a way comparable to the placing of Christ's body in the tomb and its resting there during the 'great Sabbath', while he awaited the Easter dawn. Only in this dawn and that awakening is it given to man to hear his new name, the true expression of his personality, the unutterable and undreamt of "Thou" which echoes in the depth of his heart, and gives back to him, wholly renewed, the "I" which he thought he had lost for ever. However, he will never be able to hear this "Thou," or at least to recognize it in himself, until he has heard from Jesus the glad tidings that this "Thou" is eternally heard by the Son in the bosom of the Father.

The act of faith is essentially Paschal, an act of 'passing over'. It is the passage to the further shore of the self, the act by which the believer dies completely to himself and receives a wholly new life in Christ and in God (Rom. 6:4, 10). This death, when in faith he passes beyond himself, means that a man no more regards himself, and what he knows of and discovers in himself, as the final norm either of being or of truth or of the moral law. He accepts the fact that there is something beyond his thought, his consciousness and his being. Then he bows down in adoration; or rather, in that abyss all awareness of himself is lost. If, on the other hand, he draws back and chooses like Lucifer to defy the Eternal, whatever the consequences, then he sins and falls back into an impossible dualism between God and the creature. This is the alternative that confronts every man as soon as he becomes aware of his freedom, as St Thomas Aquinas has magnificently explained (*Summa Theol.,* I-II, 89, 6).

This crucial choice between self-surrender to divine grace and the decision to retain for ever his proud independence has to be made by every human being according to the particular circumstances in which Providence has placed him, and especially in conformity with his own cultural and religious setting and the actual depth of his own self-awareness. When at last the ultimate revelation dawns upon a man, he is required to give up even the greatest treasures that he has found in himself and to go beyond the symbolic 'passing over' by which he has so far lived. He must now allow his own adoration to be lost in the theandric adoration of Jesus, God made man. Even his loss of himself in the non-dual unity must disappear in its turn in the abysses of the Trinity, in the unity of the Spirit.

Christian faith and Vedantic wisdom, mystical experience within the Christian revelation and the advaitic experience, should be compared far less in their so-called objective content than in their essential nature. Advaita is no more an idea or an intellectual discovery than is Christian faith. It is something that touches the spirit in its deepest centre, and from there takes complete control of everything in it. It is a fundamental attitude of the soul, originating at the very source of its being, a total gift of self, and a complete surrender to the mystery which has revealed itself within.

In the soul of the jñānī the Spirit of wisdom has carried his work to the furthest possible limits and has made him live his connaturality with God (see *Summa Theol.*, II-II, 45, 2) When the jñānī hears and recognizes Jesus of Nazareth, the Spirit himself will lead him directly and existentially to the very heart of the Trinitarian mystery, in an experience analogous to that which he has already known, but even more profound. In that inner place where he has his origin in God, he will hear by means of the words of revelation the very Word of the Father—who, in begetting his eternal Son, also begets him in the mystery of his adoptive sonship. He will regain his own inalienable personality in the "Thou" by which God calls him into existence in the unity of the Spirit of Love. His contemplation of the Trinity will not be of a Three-in-One or a One-in-Three which is somehow external to him. His experience of the Father and of the *ekatvam* of the Spirit will be contained in the "Thou" of the Son—the "Thou" which the Son hears and with which he responds to the Father. He will be entirely 'lost' in the Son—more completely than he ever was within his Vedantic immersion in being—and yet he will be totally and inalienably himself in his essential truth, because now he has found himself at the very heart of God. At the level of consciousness and thought he will be incapable of discerning and expressing this mystery of knowledge and love which is being revealed at the roots of his being; but this most inward experience cannot fail to penetrate the whole of his life and activity. In it the Spirit who revealed Jesus will manifest himself in the fullness of love, and this love will have recovered even in the heart of an indivisible unity, a wholly transformed relationship with other men. In this renewed contact with his brethren the Christian jñānī will live out the mystery of his response to the Father in a dependence on the Spirit now transformed into adoration.*

Invitation

One of those present said one day: "In theory one can admit that Advaita does not pose a real danger for Christian faith, and even that it could eventually prove to be an incomparable help in penetrating more deeply into the secrets of the Spirit. 'To the pure all things are pure,' everything is holy to those who are holy. Anyone who by grace has been given a realization of the truth—that inward anointing which reveals the truth (I John 2:27)—will lay hold of the truth wherever the Spirit has located it, just as a bee knows by instinct where to gather honey. But this surely presupposes a particularly solid grounding in the Christian faith, and a faith which is a living and existential experience of the God who is Truth and life?"

All agreed that a deep grounding in faith is absolutely essential for anyone who seeks to enter into close contact with Hindu thought, whether as a result of personal inclination or by the commission of the Church. It would be the height of folly to involve anyone in such a study or in such experiences without first making sure that he possessed the necessary intellectual and spiritual formation. Scholastic philosophy may have to be transcended, but first it has to be assimilated. It alone can provide the solid categories of thought which will enable the mind eventually to launch out on its own without too great a risk. The writer has to begin by learning syntax and the musician counter-point. It sometimes happens, no doubt, that India restores a sense of the sacred to Westerners who have lost it or never experienced it, and thus helps them to discover the true values of a Christianity which they had either abandoned or never really known. We have to recognize the existence of such cases and to thank God for them; nevertheless they cannot be taken as a guide for one's personal decision.

Besides, even Hindus are not invited to enter upon the path of Vedānta until they are sufficiently prepared. According to the tradition of the masters, a guru should only reveal the final secret to his disciple when he has become capable of hearing it directly in the depths of his heart. Similarly before the aspirant is allowed to begin the practice of concentration which will bring him to the silencing of all thought, and

---

*These ideas are further developed in *Saccidānanda: a Christian Approach to Advaitic Experience* (I.S.P.C.K.)

Some problems discussed

even before he is taught the preliminary muscular and breathing exercises (*asana* and *praṇayāma*), traditional Yoga lays down that he must be practising the basic virtues of patience, control of the senses, truthfulness, non-attachment, freedom from desire, etc. Experience proves the wisdom of this, and that it is extremely dangerous to play at being a yogī or jñānī before one really is such.

The Christian should be no less well prepared when he feels that he has the right or the duty to let himself be drawn into the experience of non-duality, which is at once the highest point that can be reached by the human consciousness and a state of supreme openness to the action of the Spirit. Throughout the Nagpur session great stress was laid on the necessity here in India for Christians, and above all for the ministers of the Church, to take up this preparation, both for their own sake and for that of the Church.

The fact remains that fear is incompatible with a deeply rooted faith in and love of Christ, for, as St John reminds us, perfect love casts out fear (I John 4:18). The one essential is that our confidence should be set on Christ, and not on ourselves (2 Cor. 3:4,5). Christian faith is above all a matter of confidence, *parrhesia* (Heb.10:19).

There are in general two classes of people, both among Hindus and among Christians, who are concerned with Advaita. There are those for whom it is a magnificent idea, and there are those for whom it is an overwhelming experience in the depths of the Spirit. For the first Advaita is particularly attractive in that one can discuss it endlessly, because it defies all attempts to define it in concepts. Christians can develop an equal enthusiasm for making theoretical comparisons between the formulations of Advaita and Christian dogma. This kind of interest always remains somewhat superficial; it is like the problems of pure mathematics, which are completely absorbing and yet commit one to nothing outside the conceptual order. However, such an advaita is surely not the genuine Advaita for Advaita is essentially an experience... Can an experience about which one can talk, be any longer an experience? As Lao Tse asked, "Is the *tao* that is talked about still the *tao*?"

Spiritual problems can never be reduced to problems of the intellect. The real problems that God presents to man through nature, through events, through revelation, or through the action of his Spirit in the depths of their hearts, are essentially spiritual problems, existential problems. All that can be seen, heard or even thought, belongs to the order of signs. They are means by which we express what lies in the depth of our nature and personality, by which we live our fundamental adherence to God, the offering of our souls to the One from whom we come and to whom we go. Faith is the crucial problem that God has posed to the heart of man. Like the Word of God of which St Paul speaks (Heb. 4:12), faith also is a sharp sword which pierces to the furthest recesses of our being. And Advaita, as a preparation for faith, or rather, a purification of faith, also sets a problem to the spirit. This is why no understanding will ever be possible between those people, Hindus and Christians alike, for whom Advaita is simply a philosophical system to be discussed in terms of ideas, and those for whom it raises problems affecting life itself and a man's fidelity to himself and to God.

The problem which Advaita poses for the Church is in fact an existential one. It is a providential means of purification offered to the Church by God at the very moment when her encounter with the modern technological world of the West has made her more than ever aware of the burden of her history and her deep need for a return to her spiritual roots.

Advaita does not however ask of Christianity that it should transcend itself, and set out towards a further goal beyond itself, any more than Christianity asks Vedānta to disown all that it is, in order to transcend itself and be transformed into Christianity. If there must be transcendence, then what is needed is an inward transcendence. For both Christianity and Vedānta this means that they should continue to dig down ever more deeply in search of their own living sources, should investigate ever more profoundly the secret of their own being, until each discovers in the other the presence of its own most inward mystery. This is certainly a bold assertion, but its truth will become evident to those who are willing to discover in experience the depths to which we are summoned by the Christian tradition on less than the Hindu.

The Vedānta, both in its first origin in the hearts of the rishis and also in its permeation of the entire life and thought of India, is a call from God to Christians to discover the treasures which he placed in their hearts when he called them to faith. Even now he is waiting patiently to see them bear fruit. Vedānta may be seen as an invitation to the Church to pay attention to certain fundamental aspects of

Some problems discussed

Christianity which have perhaps been underemphasized (though never entirely forgotten or lost) in the mental and spiritual climate in which she first developed.

The expressions of the Upanishads often appear harsh to those who are unfamiliar with their approach to reality. Rishis and gurus, apparently without thought for the spiritual and mental weakness of their disciples, batter them violently with their paradoxes, never allowing them to cry for mercy, until at last the awakening occurs, a throwing open of the doors, like an explosion (or even, one might say, a nuclear fission), which releases the consciousness. It is the same kind of thing on the mental level as the physical slaps and blows with a stick to which the old masters of Zen were addicted as a means of bringing their pupils to *satori* or illumination. This, to begin with, is the one thing necessary. The essential nuances and distinctions will come later, in their own time, as a kind of increment; the vital thing is to enter the Kingdom, and all the rest will be provided later as Jesus promised (Matt. 6:33).

The harshness of these statements is in fact what enables them to arouse in the souls that are ready for them an echo beyond all defining. This echo appears to rise up in the consciousness out of its own depths; it is secret, vibrant, utterly personal, however strongly the reason may try to hold it at arm's length. It is like the tolling of a bell which is scarcely noticeable at first, but gradually disturbs the peace of our slumber. The sound becomes louder and louder, as it arouses ever stronger echoes in the depths of our being. Finally it wakes us up and leaves us no choice but to leap out of bed and face the rising sun. Or it can be compared to the experience of a woman who, by means of indications at first confused and uncertain, and various unfamiliar sensations and reactions, guesses that she has become a mother. At last the day comes when the child stirs in her womb. It is true! Those who are not yet mothers may try to guess what happens and to understand it in their own way; the only ones who know are those who one day have felt the child stirring within them. Who can gainsay them?

A Duty

Advaita compels the Christian to become more and more clearly and thoughtfully aware of the dimension of interiority present in his own spiritual tradition.

Some people have thought, and indeed still think, that with regard to God and Christ the New Testament yields a theology that is merely 'functional'. From this it naturally follows that our participation in the Kingdom also belongs only to the functional, as opposed to the ontological and existential, order. Such a theology is taken for granted by those Christians who reject mysticism, but it is certainly not in keeping with the authentic spirit of the Bible and of Christian tradition*. However, it represents an attitude that is still very widespread in the Church, in practice if not in theory. Indeed Christian preaching—and likewise the formation of priests and religious—very often remains at the level of morality and the Commandments, that 'Law' in fact from which Paul, following his Lord, strove so hard to free the infant Church; or alternatively, at the level of sentimental devotions and a simple emotional piety, the Christian equivalent of the lower forms of Hindu *bhakti*.

Even when spiritual formation is given at the theological level, the underlying theology is generally far too deeply influenced by the Greek intellectualism in which it first took root and developed. It gives the impression of consisting merely of a series of logical deductions which reduce the loftiest intuitions of prophets and apostles to a set of concepts, clear no doubt, but terribly constricting, and frequently destructive of all sense of mystery. Such a theology has forgotten that if philosophy is the 'handmaid' of theology, theology itself, whether scholastic, patristic or biblical, can never be more than a servant. Its first task is to prepare the soul for an existential encounter with the living God, beyond all forms, images or concepts. Its validity will be measured by the extent to which it succeeds in integrating into itself the dimension and values of interiority which are essentially inherent in the data of revelation. Only by doing this can theology fulfil its function and lead the Christian effectively towards that experience of the deep things of God, which is his rightful inheritance as one who has been baptized and reborn in God and of God.

This is why the reading and study of the great mystics should have an essential place in the formation of priests and religious. Otherwise, how will they be able to understand anything of, for instance, chapters 14 to 17 of St John? No one has the right to make cuts in the Gospel, keeping only what serves his purspose. The study of the mystics naturally presupposes a thorough intellectual, moral and spiritual preparation, But can a complete Christian training be had for less?

Cp. J. Mouroux, *The Mystery of Time,* p. 273, note 5, and 122, note 27 : L. Malevez, *Rev. Sc. Rel.,* 1960, pp. 258ff.

Some problems discussed

In speaking of mysticism, it is surely unnecessary to explain that we are not now referring to those parapsychic phenomena which the ignorant frequently mistake for mysticism. The Spirit no doubt makes use of these at times to reveal his presence and activity, especially in temperaments of a certain type; but these manifestations are always incidental, and therefore essentially secondary. It is to the great mystics that we must turn, in order to be admitted into the secrets of divine friendship. For they alone can speak of those secrets who have passed beyond all sensible experiences (visions, auditions, and similar phenomena) to the experience of a spiritual contact stripped of all forms, which Thomas Aquinas calls the experience of wisdom, or connaturality. Examples of such great mystics in recent centuries are John of the Cross, Teresa of Avila, or Marie of the Incarnation; in the Middle Ages there were the mystics of the Rhineland, like Eckhart, Tauler or Ruysbroeck, whose mysticism is especially akin to that of India. Or one might also mention Evagrius, Gregory of Nyssa and many others belonging to the ancient Greek tradition.

Nevertheless we always have to remind ourselves that, in their expression of the supreme experience of the Christian faith, all these masters were necessarily limited by their particular social and religious conditioning. We must therefore always pass beyond the forms they used. The one essential thing to be learnt and assimilated from their teaching is the fundamental attitude of soul which they reveal to us. Man must certainly use his intelligence to draw near to God. Intelligence is a gift of God; and when transformed by grace it is raised by the working of the Spirit beyond the limitations of its natural capacity. It is the faculty that receives and assimilates revelation, and is instrumental in bringing its influence to bear on man's will and his whole life. However, the Spirit gently whispers in our heart that this heart of ours is deeper than all that intelligence can conceive or consciousness experience of it, and that it is in the depths of the heart that the ultimate mystery of God is at once hidden and made known. In so doing he invites the awakened and obedient soul which has been brought to the furthest limit attainable by a human understanding transformed by grace, to recognized and contemplate in its own depths—in the bosom of the Father—the very glory made known to us by Jesus.

As more and more Christians become deeply familiar with the mystics and their writings, the contemplative dimension of the faith which, though latent, is the present at the heart of the Church will gradually be brought to light. Then her rites, institutions and formularies, the life of her members—in a word, her whole 'epiphany', the entire 'revelation' of the Lord which by her very calling she exists to show forth in the world—will be increasingly permeated with the spirit of contemplation and interiority.

Only at this depth of interiority will be it possible for the Church to solve realistically and effectively the problems with which she is faced today by the world, by her own sons, and by the irresistible desire of all believers in Christ to form one single flock.

To turn now to the mission of the Church in India, there is no doubt that the extent to which her message spreads and is accepted will be in direct proportion to the depth of her mystical and contemplative life.

Adaptation must essentially begin from within. If this essential inner adaptation to the fundamental demand of India is lacking, then the external and sometimes showy forms of adaptation of which we hear so much today will inevitably prove to be in vain. It is not by taking over vestments, rites, musical tones and dance-steps that the Church will win a hearing in India. Such things are no doubt all to the good. It is right to make use of them; but as the Gospel says (Matt. 23:23). "These things you ought to have done, without neglecting the others." They can never be more than signs, and a sign draws its value solely from what it signifies—otherwise it remains incurably empty and meaningless, useless as salt that has lost its savour, a sham which deceives no one except those who want to be deceived. Only a Church which has fully actualized her own experience of faith and has attained to that inner depth where the authentic spiritual life of India is lived, will be capable of entering into a true religious dialogue with her. Those who are to be Christian apostles in India should therefore prepare themselves for this dialogue by serious study of the thought of India and by personal contact with her living spirituality. Their preparation will be even more effective if prayer and contemplation hold the chief place in their life. In all this they should not neglect the methods of spiritual discipline recommended by Indian tradition for quietening the senses and the mind.

The question of a 'Christian yoga' is however too complicated to be dealt with in a few lines. It will be be enough here to recall that true yoga cannot be reduced to the physical exercises with which it is too often equated in West. The essential purpose of yoga is to free the mind from its tendency to distraction by concentrating it on one point. It aims at achieving the total vacancy of thought which alone makes

Some problems discussed

possible a complete inner relaxation, and therefore a total openness to that living force that dwells at the heart of being and which Christians call the Spirit. It goes without saying that one cannot play with these things, and that normally one should not embark on such a course except under the direction of a competent master. For, once the beaten path of logical thought and the empirical consciousness is left behind, no one is able to decide for himself whether he is truly tending towards the 'fine point of the soul' or on the other hand is allowing himself to be carried away into the uncharted and dangerous world of the unconscious.

Whether he likes it or not, the Christian cannot ignore Vedānta. In the course of her earthly career the Church must encounter it—the Church of India first of all, and then in and through her, the whole Christian world. In Vedānta the Church discovers potentialities of the human spirit which otherwise could scarcely have been imagined. She also discovers the astonishing possibilities of the Indian soul, able to attain such heights even independently of the Biblical revelation. The Church's duty is clear. She must do all in her power to make it possible for Christians themselves to develop such capacities to the utmost. She must, however, see that the faithful achieve these results by the use of the proper means, and not by some roundabout path. With this in view, she should commission at least some of her children to plunge into the Indian experience of the depths of the Self, for the benefit of their brethren. Strong in their faith and their hope—the *parrhesia* referred to above—they will put themselves to school at the feet of the sages of ancient India, much as the Greek Fathers sat at the feet of the rhetoricians and philosophers of classical antiquity. When they return, their faith will have been strengthened and enriched by a new depth of experience. A kind of osmosis will have taken place in their souls between the Hindu experience of the depths of the Self and the Christian experience of the depths of the Heart of Christ. They will then be able to instruct their brothers in the royal way of the interior life, teaching them how to place themselves entirely at the disposition of the Spirit—that Spirit who searches the hearts, communicates to men the life of God, and waits only for the consent of the elect to introduce them into the very mystery of that divine life (Rev 3:20).

8
IN THE PRESENCE OF THE MYSTERY

SPIRITUAL experience, in whatever setting it occurs, should be approached only with deep reverence. It is the *mysterium tremendum*,* the essentially numinous, the Burning Bush which Moses was only allowed to approach after he had removed his sandals. It is the meeting-place of the known and the not-known, the seen and the not-seen, the relative and the absolute—or, in Christian terms, of the creature with its Creator, of the Son with the Father. It is the exclusive dwelling-place of God, to which no deva has access, neither Agni nor Vāyu nor Indra, neither sense nor will nor the reasoning mind. Brahman is beyond all this. This *tremendum*, this numinous reality, is the mystery of God himself.

To approach with reverence means, first of all, that one abandons the claim to judge or to apply one's oversimplified categories and *a priori* opinions to something which clearly transcends all ordinary powers of understanding. What right have we to pass judgment? "Only a jñāni can judge a jñāni." One can pass judgment only on what is beneath one, or at least on the same level.

Reverence also means humility: that is to say, we should very humbly seek understanding; we should give each individual the credit for his own beauty, as one of the Nagpur group very happily expressed it. This presupposes that we should at least attempt to enter into the psychology, the habits of mind and the cultural background which account for the particular forms taken by religious and spiritual experience. It further implies that we recognize that other paths may exist of which we know nothing...

Beyond all conditioning

According to the Christian revelation, this divine mystery, this *tremendum* is a 'Thou' for me, or rather, I am a 'thou' for him; indeed

---

* *mysterium tremendum*—the mystery which is at once awe-inspiring and fascinating; Rudolf Otto's definition of the numinous, the fundamental element in religious experience; see his *The Idea of the Holy*.

In the presence of the Mystery

the divine Reality addresses himself to me, and the ultimate That, *tad*, proves to be an "I". In fact, in uttering the "Thou" with which he addresses his Son, and addresses me in his Son, the Father's "I" awakens Being to awareness of itself.

Perhaps we too quickly forget that this knowledge is a pure gift of God. The substantial personality of God and my own personality, the mutual confrontation of Being between the two poles of Father and Son—and also between Creator and creature, between God and myself—are truths beyond our understanding, which the human mind cannot grasp. We cannot know them without a direct and explicit revelation from God. If a man ever comes to glimpse these truths in advance of that revelation, it can only be in a tentative and provisional way, through a kind of extrapolation or prolongation of this empirical experience of 'otherness', on which he can put little reliance. And if he has already been possessed by the experience of the atman-brahman, or at least has heard its secret from his teachers or through the Scriptures, then how will it be possible for him to take such an extrapolation seriously?

We also have no right to forget that the mental climate of both the Semitic and the Greco-Roman world was quite different from that of ancient India, and that the theological formulations of the Christian faith were therefore evolved on a completely different level of the psyche from that on which the Upanishads developed.

Since then we are obliged to approach this experience with reverence, it follows that we have to observe the *epoché* which was mentioned above (see p. 12). We have to put on one side, and as it were place provisionally within brackets, everything which is not the actual experience we are trying to understand. We should go straight to the heart of that experience, just as it is and for its own sake, until we reach its fundamental principle, so that we can discover the message that it holds for us. We need to free ourselves from our mental conditioning, refusing to pass judgment on the basis of our own philosophy and theology. The moment for the encounter will come, but only when dialogue has been established on the right wave-length. We must first of all have the patience to gather in the harvest; it can be sifted later. This way of doing things was recommended by the Lord himself in his parable of the net which first "gathered fish of every kind", and even more in his parable of the cockle (tares) among the wheat. The man who is too eager to root up the weeds is in great danger of pulling up the wheat the same time.

Our faith in Christ is strongly rooted. This is the fundamental datum, and the basis for the wonderful freedom enjoyed by the Christian, which makes it possible for him to ignore nothing, and to reject nothing, as the Īśa Upanishad puts it.

Moreover faith is itself is a mystery, and should be approached with due reverence. It is no doubt natural here to think first of the soul which has not yet received the Lord's revelation and is groping its way towards the full light. But there is also the case of those who have already received the gift of faith, but even so may sometimes experience agonies of doubt. Let him who is without sin cast the first stone, as Jesus said, if he dares to reproach such a one with insincerity or infidelity to grace.

A genuine encounter between God and his creatures, between God and me, or between myself and my brother-men, is a pure gift of grace, and this can never be repeated too often. It should never be mistaken for a conclusion based on reasoning which we would be justified in imposing on others as a matter of simple logic. We should always be on our guard against our automatic reactions when faced with something new that challenges our ingrained habits of thought. Are our 'Christian' reactions always so pure? Are they the reactions of one who simply believes—or of one who is accustomed to a particular intellectual climate? We all know how readily we condemn anything novel or unpleasing to us and, on the other hand, find a good excuse or a favourable explanation for persons or ideas with which we are naturally in sympathy.

Most of the judgments we pass on Hindus and on their religious and spiritual traditions depend on our personal and emotional attitude to them, which also unfortunately determines the degree of ease or difficulty with which we understand and assimilate those traditions.

We have no right, for instance, to blame Hindus for not appreciating the nature of sin and man's need for redemption. The knowledge of sin and of our need for redemption essentially depends on the biblical revelation, because it assumes the existence of a real encounter at a personal level between man and God. But this has nothing to do with a rational demonstration.

In the study of the Upanishads, if stress is constantly laid on their failure to refer to truths known only through revelation, it will invalidate our whole approach to them. It is quite irrelevant to the study of any particular verse to note the fact that it ignores man's sin and his need for redemption. This question should be studied essentially at the level of the intuition which underlies the thought of the Upanishads as a whole. And there again, it is not enough to establish the facts and pass judgement. We should search out the reason for this fundamental attitude, and see whether there may not still be something here from which we ourselves might profit.

We must always bear in mind the difference in cultural atmosphere between the Eastern world and the world in which Christianity developed. Allusion has already been made to the way in which the mystery is projected, as it were, 'in front of' and 'outside' the self in the typical religious approach of the West, as contrasted with the integration of the worshipper with the numinous which is characteristic of the East. In themselves these approaches are no doubt equally valid; though humanly speaking, the spirituality of the East seems to surpass anything of which the Mediterranean world in the West was capable in the religious sphere. It is true that it was in the cultural and religious setting of the Mediterranean world that God chose to reveal himself; but let us not confuse the vessel with the treasure that it contains. Christians will therefore do well to shed their own cultural and religious limitations before calling their Hindu brothers to account for theirs.

Before seeking to impose on Hindus their own ideas of God, sin and redemption, Christians should first of all allow these to be refined and purified in the pitiless light which is thrown by the Vedantic experience on every attempt to conceptualize the divine Mystery.

For example, in my personal experience of God as 'other' or of myself as a sinner, has my *ego*, my "I", really been purified of its self-centredness, its *ahaṁkāra*, as Indian tradition calls it? To set God in front of me, and myself as creature and sinner over against him, could well be—at least sometimes—only a more subtle means of self-expression, of confirming my *ahaṁkāra* and of asserting my 'I' despite all, although this experience ought to be one of complete surrender and self-abasement before the majesty of the Lord. In such cases it is all the easier to be deceived, because the subject matter is sacred and religious, and very few would be ready to suspect the presence of what psycho-analysis would call 'substitution' or 'transference'.

In the first place, then, the message of the Upanishads should be heard in a childlike spirit, free, open and eager. It should be allowed to have its effect upon us in that place "where dwells the power of Īsh, the Lord," in the heart, the temple of the Spirit which he enriches with all his wonderful gifts. These gifts, ranging from reverence to wisdom, are adapted to every need of our souls, in order to place them freely at the service of God. Let us trust the Spirit!

The Christian cannot expect the Hindu to be any more free from his natural conditioning and attachments than he is himself. Indeed, the Hindu is no less mortally afraid than his western Christian brother of experiencing the less of his empirical ego, in spite of all that he says about the need to renounce it. Hindus and Christians must learn to accept each other as they actually are, in their concrete historical situation. This is the essential prerequisite for any dialogue. The Christian who hopes to find in every Hindu a jñanī, a wholly liberated and tranquil soul, is as much mistaken as the Hindu who, after reading the Gospel, expects to find in every Christian a living embodiment of the Sermon on the Mount.

Christians can go for ever trying to persuade Hindus that man truly stands face to face with God, as a creature, as a son, and as a sinner. But India will never take this message seriously until it has been freed from the dualistic presuppositions which far too often colour our thoughts and statements about it. She will not accept as genuine the "I" that we claim to share with Christ in the bosom of the Father, until everything in us cries aloud that this "I" is totally freed from the bodily and mental ego which is superimposed on it in our empirical consciousness. Only when his "I" has been thoroughly purified and renewed in the Spirit, can the Christian proclaim with authority the Personal nature of God and the real personality of man.

This is impossible without an unqualified self-renunciation. Christian asceticism, no less than Vedantic, is inexorable in its demand for the transcending of the self. It requires a 'conversion' at the very roots of one's being. At the basis of every experience of the divine mystery there has to be a *metanoia*, conversion, and without this there can be no entering into the inwardness of that mystery. It is precisely here, as we have already seen, that the saving value of the experience of non-duality is found.

The experience of the repentant sinner is in the last analysis no different. Its roots are in the same soil. If however it seems to be even loftier, and to offer an even greater revelation of the infinity of God, this is because it involves a *metanoia* which penetrates even more deeply into the heart of man and the heart of God. It makes a man enter into the deepest recesses of his own being. In this abyss he finds no longer only a cloud, however luminous, through which the mystery shines but the living presence of the creating and redeeming God. Then he is drawn into the ultimate mystery of Being which is a communion of love, of the divine *koinonia*, indivisibly one and multiple, the non-dual outflowing of being within the depths of itself.

At the fine point of the spirit

In the Johannine *mahāvākya* or upanishads we are given the loftiest Christian expression of the experience of the mystery of God. This mystery, this absolute, dwells within us. But it is also the source and end of the cosmos, of all creation. All that lives, lives in him; all that thinks, thinks in him; all that comes to awareness of itself, awakens to itself in him.

It is in meditating on these sentences of the Gospel that the Christian truly understands the value and providential role of the Hindu experience of the ātman-brahman in the spiritual development of individuals and of mankind. The experience is in itself connatural to man, like the act of thinking and of reflecting on one's thought. It does not seem that either man's first attainment of self-awareness (the age of philosophy) or his attainment of the pure experience of the self (the age of the Upanishads) necessarily depended on any special intervention by God. Nevertheless, one cannot fail to discern the secret influence of the Spirit in the preparation and realization of these achievements and in their ever wider diffusion among the children of men. The penetration into man's ontological depths, which is realized in the Vedantic experience, certainly seems to be the highest possible preparation of the human spirit for its entry into the depths of God and for discovering there the ultimate secret of its own being.

The end of man is the vision of God; and in order to enable him to attain this end, God gave him the capacity of knowing, which he exercises at different levels. First, there are the external senses and sense-perception. Then at a higher level, but still depending on the senses, there is intelligence and the conceptual awareness of the self and the universe. Finally, crowning all, God has given him the possibility of a pure and non-reflexive self-awareness. In the course of evolution man has gradually been refined and has become less immersed in the matter from which God originally drew him. He has also progressively attained to new and ever higher levels of knowledge, reflection and awareness. But God chose India to lead the human spirit to the highest peak of consciousness.

Greece was chosen for a different mission. She had to provide the infant Church with the means of expressing in conceptual terms the essential message she had received from the Lord. Only thus could the faithful transmission of that message be assured until the end of time. The Church was wonderfully enriched by this osmosis of Hellenic wisdom and Biblical revelation. From age to age the Spirit of Understanding will continue to reveal to the faithful the treasures of knowledge enshrined in these formulations.

To the Vedantic experience, however, was entrusted the task of preparing for the work of the Spirit of Wisdom. Although older in time than the Greek discovery of the world of the intellect, it has been called later in history to make its contribution to the Church and so enter into the plan of salvation. This is fitting, for it opens up to the action of grace that level of the human psyche which seems to mark the culmination of all that man is capable of finding and realizing in himself. In the design of providence Vedānta is surely the ultimate preparation for the Gospel, for it disposes man to comprehend its most sublime mysteries in total lucidity.

In all this can be no question of the Christian trying to add an impossible 'something extra' to Vedānta, some transcendent truth of a higher order, or (to use the Indian term) to 'superimpose' upon it anything whatever. Instead, with the help of the advaitic experience itself, he must discover and make available the fullness of the treasure contained in the experience of Christian faith. It is at this point of contact between advaita and the knowledge of faith that the Christian, himself a son in the Son, attains in the unity of the Spirit to the experience of the Father, the experience of that Glory which Jesus both promised and communicated to his own. Naturally this will mean, first of all, a personal experience of being a child of the Father, a creature, a reconciled sinner. But, beyond and in the depth of this basic experience of being a son of the Father, he will also share in the very experience of the Father himself, his joy and bliss, since in virtue of being his son and heir, he has a right to share in all the Father's goods. If one may dare to express it so, it is the Father's experience which alone is eternal life and the principle and source of all that is and all that lives. It is by the communication of this experience which is imparted to me, in the communion that I have with God who is my own Father and the Father of our Lord Jesus Christ, that I myself receive being and life. But this communion with the Father is beyond all duality of thought. It is only in the experience of Being at its very source, in the awakening of Being to itself, that I stammeringly utter my response of love to the eternal appeal of the Father's love. Or rather he himself utters it in me when he utters it in his own Word, in the very act by which he is himself.

Here there is certainly an ineffable "I" and "Thou"; but there is also, simultaneously and inseparably, a non-duality, *ekatvaṃ*, that is no less ineffable. Only an awareness of this *ekatvām*, the unity of the Spirit, gives access to the mystery of the communion of love which is at the heart of that unity. And it is the Spirit of Wisdom, the divine *Pneuma* in the depths of our own *pneuma*, who makes us experientially aware of this through a connatural knowledge. This indivisible mystery of *koinonia* (communion) and *ekatvam* (non-duality) is universally present in being—between the divine Persons, between men, between men and God. But it is most perfectly revealed on earth in Jesus, the Man-God, since the whole fullness of the divine Being, the Godhead, is bodily present in his very flesh (Col. 2:9). Communion in non-duality, unity in self-communication—such is the law of being.

The final secret is the bosom of the Father, which is prefigured in the Upanishadic symbol of the *guhā*,* the most inward recess of man's heart and at the same time the furthest and loftiest heavenly abode, as the Taittirīya Upanishad (2:1) says, speaking of brahman: *nihitaṁ guhāyām parame vyoman*. It is the mystery which is inaccessible in its very proximity, close at hand and yet transcendent, at once both interior and exterior, and yet not reducible to terms of within and without, "beyond all things," as the Īśa Upanishad reminds us. But the Father reveals the inmost secret of his nature only to those whom he has chosen (cp. Katha Up., 2.23) in Jesus Christ (Eph. 1:4), the Word made flesh, the One who, as God and as man, is the essential and unique Revelation and Epiphany of the Father.

In unbroken communion

The mission entrusted to the Church is to share with all men the experience of the Spirit that is in Jesus. She has to make men realize that there is in them something deeper and more essential even than the interiority discovered by sages and mystics, a *guhā* more secret than the deepest recess of their own heart. This in fact is the abyss of the heart of Christ, which none can enter save by undergoing death—for that heart itself was 'opened' by the thrust of the soldier's lance. The

---

*guhā—See footnote on p. xiii.

Christian can only communicate this message from heart to heart, if he has first lost himself in his own depths, in this essential interiority. Here neither words nor speculations are of the slightest use. There must be a remorseless process of dying to himself, a death to the inherent dualism of the human mind and to the bondage of self-assertion which is the main obstacle to man's possession by the Spirit as foretold by Scripture. Only on this condition will the Spirit have full freedom to do his work and to bring to fulfilment all that was foreshadowed in the long preparation for the Gospel.

All Gentile sacrifices and all the treasures of the nations will then find their place in the Eucharistic and mystical offering of the Christian. With a mind enlightened by faith and the gift of wisdom he will find that all the veils which concealed the ultimate sense of symbols and prophecies have been torn away, so that he can understand all that had been written of the Lord in the Scriptures of the cosmic covenant. Finally, in his own transformed being, all the fullness will be gathered in, as he awaits the summing up of all things in Christ, in the bosom of the Father and for his glory.

A phrase that was frequently heard during the Nagpur meeting was "death and resurrection". All going to God, every entry of Christ into our life, partakes of the Paschal mystery. To draw near to God inevitably involves reconciliation, for man is a sinner; and this reconciliation is a completely free gift. But the whole history of Israel bears witness to the fact that entry into the membership of the people of God also involves a separation; this is quite clear at every step, from the setting apart of Abraham, and even earlier of Noah, until the calling of the 'Remnant'. So also the concept of 'holiness' which is central in the Bible includes the sense of being put aside for God and separated from all that is profane—in Pauline terms, of being delivered from the rule of Satan and the power of darkness.

However, it is not sufficient to remind others as from the lofty security of one's faith and settled Christian convictions, that there can be no direct passage from Advaita to Christianity. Such an attitude could only too easily be a Pharisaical means of compensation for spiritual or cultural insecurity—the very antithesis of a gift received from God and held in fear and trembling (2 Cor. 4:7 and Phil. 2:12). Jesus was not content to inform men that reconciliation with God requires the shedding of blood (Heb. 9:22); he actually shed his own blood.

It cannot be denied that there is a 'dark night' in the approach to the Gospel, just as the Israelites had to undergo the terrrible night of the Passover in which they crossed the Red Sea, when only their faith in Yahweh emboldened them to escape from Pharaoh, and as the Lord himself had to undergo the night of Agony in the garden. But India will never enter this night until those who invite and urge her to do so, have themselves entered into and experienced its pain and darkness in their own body, mind and heart. The Lord himself has led the way in doing this. He "came forth from the Father" and entered the world, not merely to point out to men the road that leads to the Father, but first of all to climb the steep path himself in the name of the whole human race and at its head. The law of substitution is at the very heart of the Christian mystery, it is the law of love itself, the supreme commandment. I am myself the price of my brother's salvation (John 15:13).

This night will be experienced by the Christian in his painful entry into the depths of the self, on behalf of those whom he represents before God. Even so did Jesus consent to allow the curse pronounced by Scripture upon the sinner (Gal. 3:13) to make itself felt in his own body and his very soul. For the Christian a double agony will be involved in the purification of his Christian faith and in the experience of non-duality. Both of these are indeed essential for him, since both are woven into the most secret fibres of his being, and express in him and through him the mystery of God and of the self. His reason may cry out that there is no transition from the one to the other, but he knows that God's gifts are irrevocable. In the depths of his being, at the point of division of soul and spirit (Heb. 4:12), he feels the anguish of this dilemma which is the final and simultaneous purification of both his experience of the self and his faith. Since the curse was laid upon Eve, there has been no entry into life without pain. The Church herself was born upon the Cross, in the agony of Christ's dereliction. The awakening to the glory of the Father in the depth of the soul is man's true birth, and he cannot escape the universal law.

It is necessary for the Christian to feel in his soul the agony of the Hindu who has heard the call of Christ but cannot see how Christianity, with all its dogmatic formulae, its institutions and rituals, can truly be compatible with the profound inner experience of which his gurus have told him, and which he may even have known for himself. At this point it is useless for the Christian to say: "Whatever the truth of this experience, I will go on believing all the same!" For that would be to refuse God's gift, and perhaps to fail in the sincerity that a man owes to God and to himself. Nor can there be any question of trying to minimize the value of the Advaitic experience, for that would be equally unworthy of a Christian and would reveal a fear that is incompatible with faith.

Jesus too was profoundly troubled in spirit when his hour had come: "Father, save me from this hour" (12:27). Yet despite his natural revulsion, he allowed himself to be brought to the Cross, for that was the very reason for his coming to his 'hour'.

India's 'hour' must first of all strike in the hearts of Christians. Only when he has allowed it to strike in him and for him, will the Christian have any right to say to a Hindu brother who still hesitates to acknowledge Christ and ask for sacramental incorporation into the People of God: "You must enter into this night, into this death."

The pain of this night is also that of the whole koinonia, the community of the Church. Salvation can only be complete when it is shared in common, in the community of the Church and of the whole universe, for there is only one Spirit, whose unity sustains all things in being. As long as a single one of my brothers is still outside the way of salvation, how can I myself consent to saved? I cannot rest at ease in my faith, so long as my brother does not yet believe. It is he and I together who must believe. I am a creature made for communion, and my faith cannot be complete until my brother shares it. I cannot help experiencing his doubt, even in the depths of my own faith. His rejection of faith must struggle with my acceptance deep within my heart, like the children who struggled in Rachel's womb (Gen. 25:22). It is as if a portion of myself also prostrates in the temple of Shiva when my brother worships there, goes on pilgrimage to Pandharpur or Kedarnath when my brother joins with the crowd of pilgrims, and is withdrawn with Śri Ramaṇa into the advaita of being. Just as Paul knew anguish of heart on account of his own pepole who had not yet drawn near to the source of grace, so the Christian of India must feel a sense of dislocation so long as all his people have not yet been integrated into the people of God.

A story from the ancient traditions of India will illustrate this. King Vipascit was being borne off to heaven by the messengers of Indra, the king the gods. On the way the servants of Yama summoned him to hell to pass a few moments is expiation of some fault that he had

In the presence of the Mystery

inadvertently committed. The king then saw and realized for himself the torments of those who were detained in hell, many of whom had been his friends and relatives on earth. So, when Dharma invited him to leave the place and proceed on his journey, he bluntly refused: "Thousands of people are suffering here. How can I leave them behind?" "They are sinners;" explained Dharma, "they have to pay for their crimes, whereas you must go to the abode of the Immortals and receive the reward of your good deeds." But Vipascit remained inflexible. His heart forbade him to go to heaven *alone*, and since hell could not detain him, all the others departed with him to the city of Indra, and so hell was emptied...

Is not this what Jesus did? And does not God expect each one of us to do the same, under pain of being tormented for ever by the terrifying question: "What have you done with your brothers?"

APPENDIX

Meetings on Hindu and Christian spirituality underlying the experience recorded in this book took place at

> Shantivanam, December 1957
> Shantivanam, December 1958
> Shantivanam, May 1960
> Almora, April 1961
> Rajpur, April 1962
> Delhi, April 1963
> Nagpur, December 1963

Two later meeting were held in Jyotiniketan Ashram in April 1964 and in January 1966. Reports of these were published in *Religion and Society* (C.I.S.R.S., Bangalore) Vol. XI (1964), No. 4 and Vol. XIII (1966), No.2.

INDEX

"Abba, Father", xiii 73, 83, 89, 91
adaptation, 110
Advaita, xiii, 19-22, 32, 46ff, 57, 62, 64, 65, 76, 90, 94-111, 118, 120, 121
ananda, bliss, 57, 86-88
Aquinas, St Thomas, 31, 101-103, 109
Ascension 72
atman, 46, 49, 53, 61-64, 67-69, 78, 90, 113, 117
Aurobindo, Sri, 22, 52
awakening, 91, 92, 100, 107, 117, 118

Benedict, St, 70, 72,
Bhagavad-Gita, 21, 58
bhakti, 15, 16, 108
Bible, 27-29, 83-84
Brahman, 46, 49-54, 57, 59, 61, 68, 70, 71, 100, 119

Church, 40, 43, 82, 98, 106, 109-111, 112
communion, *koinonia*, 28, 76, 84, 88, 117-119, 122
Communism, 96
concepts, 9, 32, 48, 62, 87, 89, 96, 105, 108, 117
conversion, 28, 116
cosmic covenant, xi, 41
cosmic religions, 4, 35, 36, 120
creation, 72, 87, 90,
Cross, 44, 121-122
Cuttat, Dr J-A, 11, 12

devas, 48-53, 56, 61
dialogue, xii, 2, 4, 6, 8, 11-12, 113-116, 119-123
dualism, 90, 96, 97, 98, 102, 116, 120
dvandva, 64, 100

Eckhart, Master, 22, 23, 71, 91, 109
ecumenism, 1, 17
ekatvam, 46, 58, 62, 66, 76, 84, 89, 100, 103, 119
epektasis, 24

epiclesis, 101
epoché, 12, 31-32, 113
eschatological, 67, 89
eschaton, 3
eternity, 92
Eucharist, 16, 36, 82-83, 120

faith, 83-94, 92, 94, 96, 101-106, 109, 111, 113-114, 120-122
freedom, 91, 98, 99-100, 102, 113
fulfilment of scripture, 38ff
fulfilment theology, 41
Fullness (pleroma), 43-44, 59-60, 62, 81, 83, 87

glory, 85-87
Gnosticism, 84, 91
grace, 44, 45, 74-75, 98, 102
Gregory of Nyssa, 24, 109
guhā, cave of the heart, xiii, 67-68, 119
guru, 47-49, 54, 55, 57, 104, 106

heart, 78, 89
hermit, 67
Hesychasm, 23
history, 18-19, 91

I-Thou, 102, 112, 119
Ignatius of Antioch, 56
image of God, 24
Indra, 52, 55, 98, 112

Jesus Prayer, 10, 23-24
jñāna, 63-65
jñānī, 63-64, 73, 90, 95, 99-103, 112
Job, 34
John, St, 30, 77-88, 93, 108
John of the Cross, St, 24, 70, 109

karma, works, 16, 21, 59, 63
knowledge, 85, 88, 98, 117

lila, 90

Index

Logos, 57, 77-83, 89
love, 83, 86-87

mahāvākya, 75, 78, 83, 117
māyā, 19, 60-67, 90
Melchizedek, 35
metanoia, 28, 116
monism, 66, 96
mūrti, 15

nāma-japa, 23
non-dualism, 9, 14, 19, 23, 42, 57-58, 62, 65, 66, 84, 92-93, 98, 105, 116, 119, 121

Old Testament, 34-41, 57
OM, 68, 81-82, 89
Origen, 96
osmosis, 95-96, 111, 118

parrhesia, 105, 111
Paschal mystery, 91, 92, 101, 102, 120
passing over (Passover), 44-45, 69-71, 91, 102, 120
Paul, St, 82, 83, 108
Paul VI, Pope, 1, 4, 29
popular religion, 56, 107-108
puruṣa 46, 71, 73, 75

Ramana Maharshi, Śri, 6, 20, 54, 65, 74, 79, 122
Rāmānuja, 21-22

Sāmkhya philosophy, 46
Sannyāsa, 65
saccidānanda, 5, 88-89
self-centredness, ahaṁkāra, 65, 115
Semitic culture, 5, 87, 113
Shankara, 19-21, 24, 100
Shiva, 36, 122
signs, 16
silence, 65, 66
sin, 19, 20, 44, 76, 98-99, 102, 114-115, 120
sonship, 9, 14, 73, 76, 84-85, 87, 118

tadvanam, 54, 57
Teresa of Avila, St, 24-25, 109
time, 89-90
Trinity, the Holy, 14, 22, 46, 58, 68, 72, 73, 84-89, 92, 93, 97, 103, 112
Tukārām 16

Umā, 52, 98
upaniṣad, correspondence, 48, 54, 78, 82-83, 93
Upanishads, the, 29-32, 46, 106, 114
Upanishads:
    Bṛihadāranyaka, 29, 46, 49, 50, 78
    Chāndogya, viii, 46, 57, 61, 75, 78
    Īśa, 29, 45-47, 58-74, 82, 83, 90, 91, 98, 119
    Kaṭha, 3, 46, 52, 74, 75, 119
    Kena, 46-58, 59-61, 67, 92, 98, 99
    Kauṣītaki, 64
    Māṇḍūkya 78, 81
    Muṇḍaka, 46, 67-69, 70, 71
    Taittirīya, 57, 119

Vatican II. 2
Vedānta, 9, 14, 20, 23, 45, 46, 60, 62-63, 67, 74, 91, 94-95, 104, 106, 111, 117, 118

Western culture, 5-6, 113, 115
Word of God, 26, 28, 31, 34, 58, 107, 119

yoga, 94, 104, 110
Yoga philosophy, 46

Zen, 106